What They're Saying About This Book.

Joe Phelps has tackled and mastered the two biggest challenges that most CEOs don't want to face – organizational structure and compensation. He tells how to build integrated communication programs, work teams, media-neutral planning, corporate culture and most of all, how to really become a client partner and provide strategic direction.

Every agency leader or would-be leader should read and use the lessons in this book.

Don Schultz, professor, founder of this country's first graduate program in IMC (at Northwestern University) and author of various textbooks on IMC.

Joe Phelps has done something that few CEOs ever do – he has let us see behind the curtain. Running one of the very few truly integrated marketing communication agencies in the world, Joe tells how he and his people were able to make this happen. His concept of "self-managed teams" is the secret organizational ingredient for producing integrated communications that build brands.

He explains not only how and why this team concept works, but also the barriers and problems that must be faced and overcome to have such an organization and produce integrated work. The book is also about culture – an agency's culture of trust, responsibility, and ownership. The only thing I don't understand is why Joe is giving his secret away. The book is sure to create a lot of competition for The Phelps Group as competitors learn how to better satisfy their clients.

Tom Duncan, Ph.D., founder of IMC graduate program at the University of Colorado. Author of "Driving Brand Value."

Joe Phelps is recognized as a top innovator in a business that innovates for a living. He's the most intellectually honest ad man I have met in my 35 years of professional life. He unselfishly shares his good ideas and without shame tells of his bad ones.

His book, Pyramids Are Tombs, makes a strong case for why small self- managed teams may be the successful structure for professional service companies in the 21st Century. It is the first organizational structure that truly allows the awesome potential of Integrated Marketing Communications to be realized

Joe's conversational style makes this organizational self-help book an easy and enlightening read. Written in bite-sized bits of information it is easy to follow and digest.

Joe's views on agency management may shock, challenge and bemuse readers, but in the end they'll be impressed with the common sense presented here.

By the end you will understand and appreciate such new concepts as "The Wall," "The WallBanger," "The Brain Bangers' Ball" and "The EyeBall."

Not just a philosopher of business practices and theory, Joe is a successful entrepreneur that puts his money where his ideas are.

I've worked in eight agencies in five countries and none were organized liked this. If I were a young person just starting in the business I would want to work in an agency just like The Phelps Group.

Gary Burandt, International Communications Agency Network (ICOM), former EVP International, Young & Rubicam

Do not read *Pyramids Are Tombs* by Joe Phelps – unless you are prepared to change not only the way that you work *but also the entire culture of your company.* Phelps describes not some *proposed* structure for a professional service company – but how a new way to conceive a company actually works at The Phelps Group. Now read the book and devour every "how-to" on the way to creating a new kind of company.

Norval Stephens Former Exec. Director, International Federation of Advertising Agencies, and EVP/COO, International, Needham Harper Worldwide

Joe Phelps' compelling description of how to build a great and enduring company is a must-read for anyone competing for customer loyalty. I've experienced his concept of self-directed teams in a full feedback environment – and found it to be powerfully effective. This book can change your management priorities and your business life in general.

Ann Graham Ehringer, Ph.D.; business owner and coach; visiting professor, Trinity College, Univ of Dublin, Ireland; former professor of entrepreneurship, USC

PYRAMIDS ARE TOMBS

Yesterday's corporate structure, like the 20th Century, is history.

Dissolve departments.
Break down the barriers.
Let your people grow!

Here's a common-sense approach with proven methods for aligning employees for ultimate success.

Joe Phelps

IMC Publishing
901 Wilshire Blvd
Santa Monica, CA 90401

Copyright © 2002 by Joe Phelps. All rights reserved.
Copyright Certificate of Registration number – TXu 1-006-069

Published by IMC Publishing
No part of this publication may be reproduced, stored in a retrieval system or transmitted in any form or by any means, electronic, mechanical, photocopying, recording, scanning or otherwise, except as permitted under Sections 107 or 108 of the 1976 United States Copyright Act, without either the prior written permission of the Publisher. Requests to the Publisher for permission should be addressed to the Permissions Department, IMC Publishing, 901 Wilshire Blvd, Santa Monica, CA 90041, (310) 752-4400, fax (310) 752-4444, e-mail: pyramids@thephelpsgroup.com.

This publication is designed to provide accurate and authoritative information in regard to the subject matter covered. It is sold with the understanding that the publisher is not engaged in rendering legal, accounting, or other professional services. If legal advice or other expert assistance is required, the services of a competent professional person should be sought.

Library of Congress Cataloging-in-Publication Data:
Phelps, Joe
Pyramids Are Tombs, Joe Phelps

p. cm. – (IMC Publishing)
Includes index
ISBN 0-9715001-0-X

Library of Congress Control Number: 2001096765

TABLE OF CONTENTS

Acknowledging Those Who Helped.

Most people believe axioms like "the more you give, the more you get." However, fewer people seem to believe this is true in the business world.

This book is dedicated to all who have influenced and supported me in my belief that our business associates rise to their highest levels when given freedom to do as they wish – and are simply held accountable to their own goals.

To my deceased mentors and influencers: Red Douglas, Father Kevin, Bob Humphreys, Dale Carnegie, Norman Vincent Peale and Ed Deming. To the living: Ann Ehringer, Ben Jack, Don Schultz, Tom Duncan and Bill Schultz.

To those who have believed enough in our agency's sometimes seemingly wacky concept to spend more than 15 years of their lives supporting and helping to develop it: Sylvia Phelps, Glenn Schieke, Joe Hartnett and Judy Lynes.

Thank you Joe Hartnett for providing the title, *Pyramids are Tombs*. To Judy Lynes, Jerry Derloshon, Kristen Bergevin, Nancy Padberg, Chrisie Scott, Tom Rector, Natalie Franks,

Jay Metzger, and Cynthia Clotzman for their edits. To Mike Rose, Mike Cunningham, Julie Miyahira, Randy Brodeur and Mike Peterson for the design and production. And to Bill Threlkeld for driving the project down the home stretch – otherwise I'd still be tinkering with it.

To all other associates at The Phelps Group who are helping to build an agency whose purpose is to promote only those products that enrich the lives of those who buy them and to create a working environment that fosters trust and personal freedom.

To our deserving clients, who've been our partners in helping us realize this concept and our success.

And to my son and daughter, Douglas and Emilie, who are frequently my father and mother. I learn so much from you.

Joe Phelps

About the Title, Pyramids Are Tombs.

The premise of this book is that organizations with top-down, command-and-control management (and organizational charts shaped like pyramids) are the dinosaurs of the service-oriented, information age in which we live.

Those organizations are not built for the speed necessary to compete today.

They do not draw on the brainpower of the entire organization.

They are not built to provide the freedom and flexibility required and demanded by today's knowledge workers. They represent the ways of the past – just as the Pyramids of Egypt are structures dedicated to preserving the ways and relics of a time long ago.

This book may provide a modern-day Rosetta stone to guide those searching for a better way to organize a professional services firm.

This Book's Purpose.

If you find the right people, make them accountable to their own goals, and provide a healthy working atmosphere, you simply need to get out of the way so they can get their job done.

There is a new and better way to organize professional service companies. And there's considerable evidence pointing to the fact that *self-directed, client-centered teams* are the optimum model for today's knowledge workers.

Pyramids are Tombs was written first and foremost to help align our associates at The Phelps Group – so that, as we grow and as time passes, we may have a common understanding of who we are, where we're going, how we're getting there and why we're doing it this way.

However, in our ultra-fast, hyper-competitive service economy, we believe almost every business can benefit by applying the principles practiced here at The Phelps Group. The basics we learned from years of trial and error are right here in this book. Feel free to replicate the culture or processes in areas where you believe they will improve your organization. We'd be honored.

The following is a note to Joe Phelps from Eric Wentworth, an associate of The Phelps Group when he wrote:

> To most of the world our *self-directed*, client-based teams concept is new and even fairly radical in comparison to traditional client/agency relationship models. *Our method addresses the world as it has evolved in the latter part of the 20th century.* It focuses on principles that are now becoming recognized as essential to the human spirit and doing good business in a responsible, humane manner.
>
> With all the news of downsizing, terrorist bosses, people being fired because they have accumulated too much in their pension funds, CEOs who take hundreds of millions in compensation – often at the expense of the rank and file employees, the compassionate and human approach that is exemplified by the methods we practice at The Phelps Group should have a large, receptive audience.

There's a sea change in the marketing communications industry. With the proliferation and penetration of new media vehicles (Internet, satellite TV, wireless devices, PVRs) and because our individual screening devices are more evolved and more difficult to pierce, the old ways of reaching us just aren't good enough. *Integration* of messages can add focus and power to the message delivery. Truly integrated campaigns have significant advantages over traditional advertising and PR agency approaches.

This fundamental change is occurring in other professional service industries such as accounting, law and insurance. The same principles apply across these service industries.

This book shows the specific methods and successful results of delivering customer service through self-directed, client-based teams. And it uses The Phelps Group's work in integrated communications as a vehicle for demonstrating how this organizational model works.

Introduction.

As the speed of business continues to increase and knowledge workers demand more freedom of movement, the old methods of top-down supervision are quickly becoming outmoded.

At every spurt of your company's growth you may find you're making more decisions in less time about things you're less informed about. So you may be wondering how to organize and adapt to keep up with the changes in people's attitudes and advances in technology.

The workplace and methods of communicating are changing dramatically. So it makes sense that methods of organization will have to change dramatically, too.

Pyramids Are Tombs explains how you can organize to give people the things they need as human beings, while using technology to maximize their productivity. This is not simply textbook business theory. It's documentation of how a real company has organized self-directed people in self-directed teams around their customers in client-based teams. It explains how they have abolished functional departments in order to maintain customer focus and balance in the lives of their associates.

Going For the A+.

Remember that one course in school you loved the most? You did all your homework, took careful notes in class and studied hard for the tests. And you aced it.

The Phelps Group is that special "course" for us. Our mission is to do *great work for deserving clients*. And we've been building this company with a tremendous amount of care. We believe we've found a better way to organize – to align all participants to have a better chance of realizing their potentials. Therefore, we've tried to capture the essence of who and what we are in this book, so that others may learn from us and, in turn, help us refine our processes even further.

Written primarily for people in service companies, the ideas, processes, and applications in the book will apply most specifically to professional service organizations such as marketing communications, architecture, accounting, law and insurance firms. So, in referring to "companies" we're generally referring to those types of organizations.

How the Book Is Structured.

The concept of The Phelps Group can be summarized as:

Self-directed, client-based teams
In a full-feedback environment
Delivering integrated marketing communications
In the spirit of our mission
To achieve our vision

The "thrusters" on our logo represent the alignment of these five elements.

That's the template for our thinking. So this book is organized in that same order.

Part One: Self-directed, client-based teams, suggests that pyramid-type, multi-layered organizations comprised of functional departments are, in many cases, obsolete – and explains why self-directed teams are right for these times. It provides a working blueprint for how to organize *around* clients.

Part Two: In a full-feedback environment, describes the feedback mechanisms needed to balance the otherwise independent teams.

Part Three: Delivering integrated marketing communications, explains how marketing communications can best be integrated.

Part Four: In the spirit of our mission, explains how our specific mission gives meaning to our work and instills trust within the company.

Part Five: To achieve our vision, describes our vision of where we see ourselves going and how we've aligned the elements to maximize success.

Our goal for this book is to paint a clear picture of how individuals, aligned with the goals of a company, deployed in self-directed teams and operating in a full-feedback environment, are better able to reach their full potential, provide their employers with a greater return on their investment, and deliver excellent client service.

This book is a candid look inside The Phelps Group to see just how the above theory is playing out in reality. We hope it articulates our processes clearly so that other service organizations can benefit from the investment we've made in inventing and building our company.

Note: This book will never be complete. A philosophy of continuous improvement means that it will be in a constant state of evolution. All suggestions for edits and additions are welcome. Please address them to:
pyramids@thephelpsgroup.com.

Part One:
Self-directed teams

Self-directed teams

Why a New Organizational Model Is Needed.

Teams and teamwork are the mantras in American business today – and rightfully so. There has to be a better way to work than through the slow-moving, politically motivated departments within most of today's corporations.

There are basically three ways to organize a service company:

- Function-based departments
- Matrixed departments (function-based departments whose members also report to customer-based teams)
- Self-directed, customer-based teams

Before examining these three organizational models in more detail, let's look at how the leverage in the marketplace has shifted from the manufacturer, to distribution, to the consumer during the past century.

This will serve as a foundation for the argument that the type of organizational model that best serves today's market is no longer the autocratic, top-down, pyramid model that most companies can't seem to abandon.

Fact: Since the industrial revolution began, leverage has moved steadily from the manufacturer to the distribution channels to the customer.

To illustrate, consider Henry Ford's famous quote: "You can have any color Ford you want as long as it's black." The *manufacturer* was in control. The early 1900s were the days of, "If we make it you'll buy it." The consumer didn't have a lot of choice.

Contrast that with someone walking into a coffee shop today and asking for a medium-sized, half caf, ½ decaf with 1% milk!

In the first half of the century, leverage moved to the distribution channels – first to the railroads and then to the wholesalers and retailers. These middlemen would (and still do) tell the manufacturer what they will stock in inventory. The retailers represent the consumer to the manufacturer. But the manufacturer, in these instances, responds to channel demand, not direct consumer demand.

During the 50s and 60s, Sears built a huge customer base because they were able to control a great number of factories. To get an understanding of just how powerful retailer leverage can be today, talk to any manufacturer who supplies products to Wal-Mart. Wal-Mart dictates virtually everything right down to the manufacturer's margins. The manufacturer does it according to Wal-Mart's specifications, or they lose the opportunity to distribute through America's most dominant retailer. They imply, "It's Wal-Mart's way—or the highway."

Over the past decade, the end-consumer has been given more choice of where (s)he can buy. In addition to retail outlets, catalog sales have flourished with the proliferation of in-bound telemarketing call centers, making it faster and easier for people to order from catalogs. And starting with the launch of the World Wide Web protocol in 1994, Internet e-commerce has grown dramatically, and most people agree that the more it grows, the more it *will* grow. Initially, manufacturers were reluctant to sell directly to the end user via the Internet. But those barriers are falling as manufacturers and their distributors learn to work together with this new medium.

It's obvious the Internet is just one more channel for the consumer. The more choice of distribution outlets a consumer has, the less leverage the retailer has, the less leverage the manufacturer has and the more things *must* be done the way the consumer wants them done.

Three Ways To Organize.

With that in mind, let's look again at the three methods of organizing a professional service company:

- Function-based departments
- Matrixed departments whose members also report to customer-based teams
- Self-directed, customer-based teams

Any one of these models will work. Success for these models will be determined by how well they are executed. However, my contention is that *self-directed teams* are more in tune with the needs of people today and the clients they serve. Everything else being equal, self-directed teams will outperform the other models.

A little more detail on each model:

Function-based departments

This model was born of the industrial revolution. It worked best when the factory was "king." It focuses on doing things in ways that appear to be best for the *supplying* company, making function-based departments even less appropriate for today. This method too often results in doing things in the way that's best for the departments – not necessarily the customer. It's epitomized by the answer to a customer request being something like, "We don't do it like that in this department." Or, "I don't handle that, let me transfer you to the right department." (Don't you feel a little frustrated by simply reading that line?)

Of all parts of the supply chain, the best place for the function-based department model is in the factory. However, Edward Deming, the "father of self-directed teams in modern times", showed Japanese car manufacturers the advantages of getting rid of the quality control department and making the assemblers themselves responsible for their own work. When he brought this team-based model to Detroit, the Ford Taurus was its first test case. The Taurus set Ford's record for the fewest defects and went on to become America's most successful car model.

Amazing, isn't it, that the self-directed team model is more accepted in the automotive "rust belt" than it is by professional service firms where knowledge workers demand the most trust and freedom?

An example of a professional service firm organized in *function*-based departments would be a law firm that's organized with departments for litigation, estate planning, real estate, bankruptcy and criminal law. Or an accounting firm organized with departments for auditing, taxes and management consulting.

Matrixed Departments

When departments and teams are matrixed, individuals report to two masters, the internal department head and the client-based team. This type of organization recognizes the need to organize around a client's needs. But it's not totally committed to the concept. And there are distinct disadvantages to not going all the way to purely self-directed teams.

Matrixed teams are stuck in an inefficient, anxiety-producing purgatory – halfway between function-based departments and the truly client-based teams whch are responsible for every aspect of the work they do for a client.

Example: *Marketing communications* agencies today are most commonly organized with a creative department, a media department, an account management department, a public relations department, a direct marketing department, etc. The people in these departments officially report to their department or division manager. Yet they work on specific accounts, so they are also on those informal client-based teams. The question always arises: "Am I working for my department manager or the client?"

A Roman proverb states: "If a slave has three masters, he's a free man." This applies in principle to having two masters as well. Who is prioritizing the tasks when you have two masters? There's a built-in conflict of interest.

Another adage that applies here is, "Everyone's responsibility is no one's responsibility." When a job goes through a department, and it's the ultimate responsibility of the department head, it can't also be the ultimate responsibility of the specialists working on it. More conflict of interest.

Self-directed, customer-based teams

Considering the fact that the word "team" is used a lot when referring to teams in a matrix system, let's clarify. In this book, when I speak of "teams," I'm referring to self-directed, client-based or project-based teams, whose members live and die by their own sword, and do not report to department heads.

This book champions this model. Companies using this method of organization are rare. We believe the reasons for this lack of acceptance center around three obstacles:

- Overcoming the inertia of past traditions
- Opposition that typically arises from department heads who perceive their power as stemming from an individual profit center
- Lack of awareness that it has proven to be an effective model for organizing a professional services firm.

The best proof we can offer for this in the service industry is The Phelps Group. According to various industry experts, The Phelps Group is an excellent example of this model in action. It's working, and *Pyramids are Tombs* was written to explain why it's successful.

That being said, we know there are exceptions to every rule. There is no *one* single organizational structure that will fit all professional service firms. However, we're passionate about the advantages offered by the pure self-directed teams model – so please forgive me as we sing its praises throughout this book.

Task-Oriented Departments
Pure Pyramids: Work in separate departments.

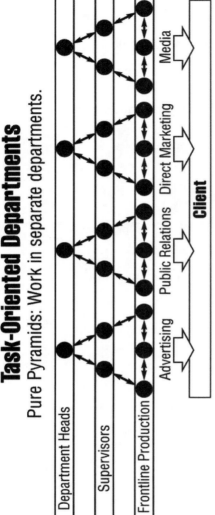

Department Heads

Supervisors

Frontline Production

Advertising   Public Relations   Direct Marketing   Media

Client

Matrix Organization
Work in departments, coordinate with others.

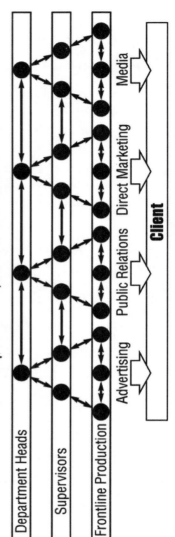

Department Heads

Supervisors

Frontline Production

Advertising   Public Relations   Direct Marketing   Media

Client

Purely *task-oriented* departments suffer from the least amount of interdisciplinary communication. This improves with the *matrixed organization*, but there's conflict of interest due to people reporting to both the department head and the client.

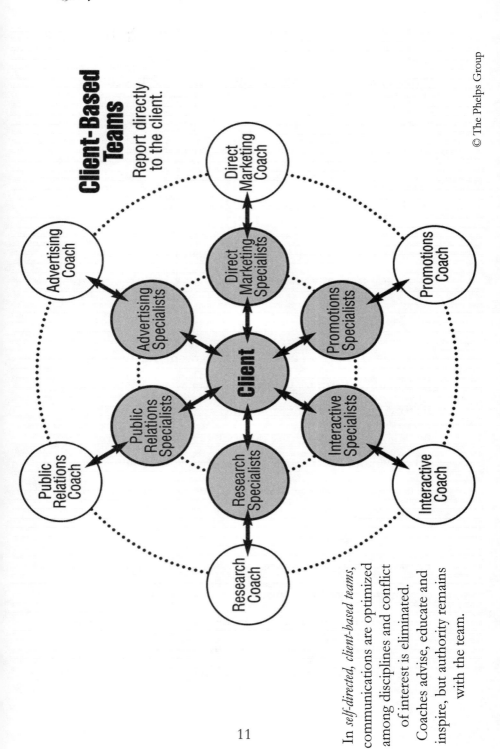

Client-Based Teams

Report directly to the client.

Direct Marketing Coach

Advertising Coach

Direct Marketing Specialists

Promotions Coach

Advertising Specialists

Promotions Specialists

Public Relations Coach

Public Relations Specialists

Client

Interactive Specialists

Research Specialists

Interactive Coach

Research Coach

In *self-directed, client-based teams*, communications are optimized among disciplines and conflict of interest is eliminated. Coaches advise, educate and inspire, but authority remains with the team.

11

Lessons From History.

The Evolution to Self-directed, Customer-based Teams

Sometimes it's easier to understand where you are if you know where you've been. This first chapter takes a quick look back to the industrial revolution to put today's working environment in perspective.

Someone once told me, "The important thing about education is what you remember after you've forgotten the facts."

As a boy growing up in the South, I committed to memory the significant names, dates, and places which shaped U.S. history. While I've long since forgotten most of the specific facts I regurgitated during pop quizzes and exams, what I do remember – the processes, the changes and human movements forward – have helped me understand larger issues affecting societal change.

For instance, Eli Whitney's breakthrough invention of the cotton gin might be regarded as the flash point for the Industrial Revolution. The year that Eli made history with his invention has faded from my memory. However, I am aware of the significant amount of stress the Industrial

Revolution caused, driving a wedge between people in the agricultural regions in the South and the industrial regions to the North.

That stress resulted in the outbreak of the Civil War, one of the most devastating internal national conflicts in all of history. The North was further along the industrialized trail and not as dependent on slave labor to fuel its economic growth. So, the North moved more quickly to abolish slavery. The South, meanwhile, without the same resources, clung desperately to the only way of life it knew. In the final analysis, the Civil War was not just about slavery. It was about adjusting to sweeping changes in the economics of a nation – changes that were forced upon it by technological advances.

The Industrial Revolution set up a myriad of other societal tensions such as child labor and violent strikes. Some of these problems were solved by third party collective bargaining in the 1930s.

Then, in the 1960s, the "Great Society" brought national attention to race, sex and age discrimination.

Fast forward to the present and we see tremendous stress resulting from the current Information Revolution which is taking place at the dawn of the Communications Age. This stress hasn't caused an overt war, as in the past. Rather, today's stress is a silent struggle for freedom as we attempt to break away from the schedules and ways of life that were developed for the manufacturing-driven Industrial Age.

Life in the later years of the industrially driven economy was organized in five, eight-hour workdays per week, with two weeks of vacation and one-income households with stay-at-home spouses. This outdated model is no longer relevant.

The essence of this book is to show a new way for service organizations, and the people within them, not just to cope – but to thrive – in the Communications Age.

More Lessons From History.

At the height of the Industrial Revolution, some of the most financially successful capitalists were known as "robber barons." These capitalists used their company-owned land and capital (factories, railways, company stores, equipment, etc.) as leverage to control a labor force that had minimal leverage because they owned no capital. Long hours, dangerous and unhealthy physical conditions, child labor, lack of job security and discrimination were the norm for the rank and file worker.

The situation was out of balance. Its backlash resulted in the rise of labor unions and the development of Marx's fundamental belief in state-owned, rather than privately owned property, establishing the Communist version of socialism as a political and economic ideology.

Obviously, neither of these systems, situated at extreme opposite ends of the bell curve, was the answer. Capitalists often abused their power. Employees developed distrust for management. Pure socialism, on the other hand, disincentivized workers by placing them in situations where they could not directly derive a benefit from their efforts.

Labor unions, and the often corrupt misrepresentation for which they're known, were not the answer either. They were (and still are) makeshift approaches to solving symptoms, rather than a treatment for the underlying problems.

Robber baron-controlled capitalism, pure socialism, and labor unions were all extreme solutions. Yet these extremes provided the tension needed to evolve the workplace as an ongoing lab to encourage new and better ways to live and work.

A More Balanced Approach.

Over the years, U.S. social programs propped up the system to provide increased levels of support and care for the disabled and elderly. The programs were a way of blending the opposing theories and practices of socialism and capitalism into a more balanced and potentially more equitable approach.

Other balancing mechanisms that have evolved are communications and mobility. They've both given individuals greater leverage, which allows more freedom of choice. First, improved communications have helped workers find out about other employment opportunities. Just look at the dramatic rise of the use of the Internet for recruiting and job searching. Secondly, the improved transportation infrastructure has made it easier to move to other areas to take these jobs.

These two factors have helped equalize the balance
between individuals and the companies they work for. Two
obstacles have been removed from the path of a free-
floating market:

- Ignorance of other opportunities
- An inability to capitalize on them

Therefore, in the last half of the 20th Century, the world,
and in particular the Communist block countries, watched
as America's free enterprise economy pulled further and
further into the lead. And overall, as individuals, we
maintained, and even increased, our freedom.

Safer working conditions, health insurance, company-
sponsored right-to-work policies, paid time off and
generally better working conditions are now the norm.

Pyramids Are Tombs.

Enter the Communications Age – the age of the knowledge worker, the computer and the Internet.

Assets of today's companies are increasingly located between employees' ears. Major investments of companies, therefore, are in the education of the workforce. These assets can walk at a moment's notice. They can go to work for a competitor for the same and sometimes better wages and benefits. So now who has the leverage?

This balancing of power is requiring companies to offer more than just a wage. And it is creating a world in which *Pyramids Are Tombs*. In this new world, top-down, multi-layered management structures are inadequate when it comes to retaining, motivating and maximizing the potential of the new knowledge workers.

A Relentless Search to Maximize Human Potential.

Companies that are organized in self-directed teams, rather than top-down hierarchical structures, empower individuals to exercise a greater degree of initiative while assuming more personal responsibility.

People in the first-world nations have evolved from being *need* driven, to being *desire* driven. We have what we need to survive.

So with our food, clothing, shelter and security needs taken care of, we're moving up one more rung on Maslow's hierarchy of needs toward self-actualization.

Maslow's Hierarchy of Needs

Job Satisfaction Is Job # 1.

With the free market determining the labor costs (salaries) in most products and services, the most important value-added component a company can offer its people increasingly will be job satisfaction.

Extensive research has been done on what's important to us in our jobs. The conclusions of most studies are that the main components of job satisfaction are:

- *Recognition for a job well done* – Mark Twain said he could live for two months on a good compliment.
- *A healthy working environment* – clean, well-lit, adequate space; the proper equipment; and a space inhabited by people who care and who communicate in an honest, timely fashion.
- *Meaningful work* – trading your time in life to help achieve something worthwhile.
- *Responsibility* – a belief that people are responsible for their own actions, and indications that they are trusted.
- *Accountability* – a feeling of ownership of outcomes; a sense of the proverbial buck stopping with every single person and not in the lap of someone far down the line.
- *Equitable compensation* – linked not to longevity or rank, but to performance; being treated like partners; possible equity in the business can be important.
- *The chance to learn* – opportunities to grow into more significant positions with greater responsibility and

ultimately, to increase one's value to the organization.

- *The chance to do great work* – not just work that meets minimum standards and expectations, but quality work: A+ work!
- *Understanding* – knowing how the work relates to the realization of the overall goals of the business.
- *The chance to work with interesting, motivated, responsible people* – whose personal and professional goals are in alignment with one's own.

Two other elements that will continue to become even more important are job flexibility and personal freedom.

Now, take just a moment to review the list again. It becomes obvious that the concept of a self-directed worker deployed on a self-directed team is a natural system for making sure many of these needs are met.

As you read further, you'll find even more evidence in support of the contention that the needs outlined above are satisfied by deploying people in self-directed teams.

Let Freedom Ring.

Freedom, expressed as time and place – where I want to be when I want to be there – has to do with: flexible time to take care of other life chores as needed; experiencing more of the joys of family, friends and new challenges; the flexibility to work from virtually any place at any time; and to be connected to families and communities more than ever before.

We can have that flexibility now, because technology finally allows us to sever the tether from our offices and desks, yet stay in touch with our teammates.

Professional service people often are thinking about their work challenges in the shower, on the freeway and, too often, when they should be listening to their spouse and children. They're working, or have the potential to work around the clock. This is a far cry from the "leave it all at work when the whistle blows" mentality of the factory workers and, to a great extent, many of the white-collar workers of modern day bureaucracies.

The combination of this desire for freedom, the flexibility made possible by communications technology and the "always on my mind" mental work calls for an organizational system that's at the other end of the spectrum. The departmentalized, "always in your face" pyramidal hierarchies invented for factory work are simply outdated.

Let's Trust Each Other.

The continuous pressure of solving work problems, regardless of where one is physically, sets up the need for a counterbalancing tension release. One release can be *flexibility*, in terms of when and where someone works. Granting this flexibility requires *trust*.

What's wonderful about human nature is that trust begets trust. If you trust me, I'm much more likely to trust you. The more we trust each other, the better we communicate. The better we communicate the more productive we are together. It's either an upward spiral, or a downward spiral, depending on the level of trust.

Leadership's purpose, after setting the mission and vision for the company, can almost be distilled to:

- Find the right people.
- Provide them with the resources they need to do their job.
- Hold them accountable to their own goals.
- Show *trust* by getting out of their way and allowing them to do what they've committed to do.

This cultural mindset will improve employee retention by enhancing their commitment to the organization, as opposed to their merely "obeying" in order to earn money.

Here's an example of how we show trust at The Phelps Group. We say, "We only hire adults." This means we don't have to tell people when to be at the office, what to wear or how to treat each other. It has minimized the number of written policies and is a reflection of how much we trust our associates.

Our associate Ed Chambliss (who received the top IMC graduate student award when he received his MBA at Colorado University) said it this way in a memo to me:

> "I overheard two ladies talking about their company's travel policy. The policy (from a large Hollywood studio) was amazing. It actually dedicated six single-spaced pages to travel policy, including a chart indicating which level executive is allowed to fly First or Business Class (if the flight is over seven hours, of course.) I also caught a glimpse of an entire paragraph outlining how unused airline tickets must be returned to a participating travel agency.
>
> This experience crystallized for me the difference between The Phelps Group and other companies where I've worked.

It's the way our organization treats us like responsible adults. In contrast, many companies treat their employees like children – forcing management to act like parents.

We're all responsible adults who, treated as such, will work together to get things done.
To me, this is the focus (and benefit) of the way we do things here. Client-based teams are just common sense. They allow us to be adults. And, given that opportunity, we'll use our common sense to get the problem solved. Isn't that what it's all about?"

Well said, Ed.

It's About Alignment.

Alignment exists when individuals know their contribution to the group is a contribution to their personal mission.

For alignment to exist, there must be an absence of conflicts of interest between the individual, the team they're on, the company they're with, the clients they work with and the suppliers who support them. Now *that's* a tall order.

Alignment is central to our philosophy at The Phelps Group. The five "thrusters" in our logo are moving upward and in parallel formation. They symbolize the alignment of our basic tenets and business model – summarized in the five sections of this book – self-directed teams, in a full-feedback environment, delivering IMC, in the spirit of our mission, to achieve our vision.

The thrusters also illustrate a philosophy influenced by Dr. Ed Deming's work. This philosophy states that processes are the key to a company's success. The closer a process is to the *beginning* of the overall system, the more important it is – such as those related to the recruitment of associates. If a company recruits smart, motivated, team players (visualize them as rocket engines), and these people's personal missions are in alignment with the company's, then they're like multiple rocket engines strapped to the company mission, propelling the company upward toward its vision.

These five associates came to our Halloween party as the "thrusters" in our logo, chanting in unison, "We have a vision. We are on a mission." Scary.

A Healthy Culture Fosters Alignment.

To foster alignment there must be a *healthy company culture* that attracts the right people and allows them to work at their highest level of performance.

To accomplish this, we believe in:

- Publishing our company's tenets: values, mission, vision and methods of operation.
- Setting performance standards.
- Recruiting people to match our high standards.
- Ensuring that all associates understand and commit to the tenets and standards.
- Encouraging individuals to develop their individual performance action plans.
- Measuring individual progress toward these commitments.
- Recognizing individual and team success.
- Terminating underachieving associates or ones who are not aligned with our philosophies.

Here are some examples of how our philosophies helped build our culture:

When our agency was less than 20 people and we divided that group into client-based, self-directed teams, there was natural resistance because all of us had been conditioned by traditional department-oriented backgrounds to believe that each discipline should have a director responsible for the work in that department.

As we grew to have multiple art director/writer teams, there was pressure to have a creative director. (The same was true in the other disciplines at the agency.) However, we were adamant about using our more experienced associates as *coaches* to help inspire and guide, but leaving the final decisions and responsibility with the teams. As CEO, I was under constant pressure to revert to the old "department/director" model.

That pressure has now disappeared. The number of associates has grown dramatically and our success has proven the model as valid. The culture is now strong enough to attract people to us *because* of our "no departments" philosophy. When our new people's previous conditioning influences them to revert to the old ways, the people around them provide peer pressure to bring them back into alignment.

For example: if someone is not subjecting their work-in-progress to the feedback of associates – whether it be on their team or agency-wide – it's their peers who most often remind them. That's the power of the culture bringing them into alignment. It's typically just a matter of helping them to *remember*, not one of convincing them of the values they committed to when they came aboard.

A basic tenet of our mission — *a healthy working environment* — is supported by the premise that open, honest and timely communications will solve most problems. Our constant vigilance to uphold this tenet, combined with our selective hiring processes, and a flat (non-political) organizational model, has helped create an agency that people inside and outside regard as a group of loving and caring individuals. Now, because that's become an important part of our company personality, when anyone exhibits behavior outside the norm, they feel the peer pressure to re-examine their actions and come into alignment with the company culture.

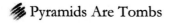

New Times Call For New Solutions.

All these changes in factors affecting the workplace, the family, communication, transportation, the balance between employer and employee leverage, and people moving up the hierarchy of needs, have created the demand for a new way of organizing companies.

One of the basic premises of this book is that the truly self-directed team – working in a robust feedback environment – is the answer to how knowledge workers can best be organized. This pure team approach may well be the preferred method of work in the Communications Age.

Why Small Teams Work Best.

Too far left: Karl Marx, in his *Communist Manifesto*, recognized and lauded the desire of people to work as a group for the good of all. However, he underestimated the individual's primary drive to work for his/her own good.

Too far right: Adam Smith, in his *Inquiry into the Nature and Cause of the Wealth of Nations*, recognized the productive power of free enterprise. But during the Industrial Age, businesses required such heavy capital investments (land, buildings, large machines) that the individual worker lost too much leverage.

Right down the middle: Conversely, small teams provide a happy medium between the two extremes. They are small enough to make "one for all and all for one" real and believable to the participants. They contain the rewarding social element of camaraderie, which is so necessary for most people to feel their work is fulfilling.

Participants on a small team can see the fruits of their individual efforts. They can see the actual work they've performed. There's no place to hide on small teams like there is in a bureaucratic division or department of a large

34

company. So one's personal contribution can be measured. And one can be duly rewarded for exceptional work.

Personally, I believe that humanity is evolving toward a state of enlightenment in which the balance of the primary drive between benefiting others vs. benefiting one's self is shifting. That shift will take generations. And it will be free enterprise that allows the satisfaction of the more basic need levels and allows mankind to move up its hierarchy of needs toward true self-actualization.

How Big Can a Small Team Be?

There's no *exact* answer to the question of what is the optimum team size. It depends on human factors, such as the make-up of the individual players. For example, how well do they communicate and how generous are they with praise and credit for success? It also depends on how many different skills are needed for the tasks at hand.

History has proven that there are optimal sizes for organizations, and in this context, teams. If the team is too small, there's not enough critical mass or variety of talent. If the team is too large, it becomes slow and the direct personal payback is diminished. For example, have you ever stepped out on a softball field with 15 players already on the turf? The feeling is usually: "There's no room for me here. They don't need me. It'll take me forever to get up to bat."

There are guidelines for setting team size. Think in terms of the games we invent for entertainment. Our sports teams, for example, are typically made up of 5-12 people. If the team is too small, the power of the feeling of group victory is diminished. If the team is too large, people begin to lose sight of their individual contribution, and the chance of building deep relationships is diminished.

Think in terms of how many disciplines are needed, and how many specialists in each discipline.

Consider carefully the balance between having a specialist complete an entire task vs. dividing it into higher and lower levels to be divided among less- and more-experienced people.

Software is automating so many left-brain tasks that it's becoming more practical to allow a higher salaried person to do the entire task without delegating to others. This alone is allowing for smaller teams. The smaller the team the fewer "batons" are passed in the race to completion of a project. Smaller teams can usually change directions more quickly. They see more results of their individual efforts. Individuals can see their true vision come to fruition as they move from conception through execution without interference or compromise with others.

Self-directed Teams

Smaller teams have many advantages. The *disadvantages* of fewer members can be offset by insuring two important elements:

- The quality of the individuals on the team.
- The amount and timing of the feedback they receive on their work in progress.

Frederick Reichheld of Bain & Company, a research firm, wrote in the October, 2001, issue of Harvard Management Update in his article on employee loyalty, "…the military has learned that the essential management device that makes beliefs and desires practical and operation is the small team in which individual soldiers operate. Small units, made up of 5-10 soldiers, provide clear visibility and accountability. Everyone's role is vital because there is no slack, and even in chaotic battle conditions, rapid communication and coordination are still possible."

As to the effect a team's size has on *loyalty*, Bain's research reveals that at least half the teams in American companies are too large to foster superior loyalty. It concludes that small teams have the highest levels of employee loyalty, and that on average, a team of seven or fewer scores 15 percentage points higher on employee loyalty than teams of more than 25.

Cynthia Clotzman, an associate and our Customer Relationship Management (CRM) coach articulated her experience in working with teams of various sizes and skills in the following illustration:

12 person team:

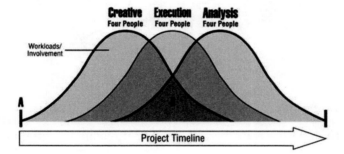

"When a team is large – 12 people, for example – they often have 4-8 members who are not heavily involved throughout the process. I have found that if 'mini-teams' are brought in throughout a project's life, less people sit in on meetings that don't affect them, and they are able to work on other projects where their skills are more needed at that time."

Sand Hills.

My friend Steve Woolley once demonstrated to me a natural physical phenomenon that relates to this subject of pyramid-shaped structures.

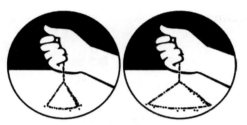

Pyramid-shaped structures naturally want to flatten as they grow in size.

He took a handful of sand and poured it into a little pyramid. As the sand rose higher and it reached a certain point, the structure would shift and the sharp pyramid shape would collapse into a flatter form. The pile was stable when small and low. As it grew higher, it became less stable. At some intermediate stage the pile had a few trickles and the beginnings of instability. As it continued to grow, it became catastrophically unstable. Small movements or trickles triggered collapses.

There are obviously parallels between the growth and resulting instability of a pile of sand and the growth of an organization. Although it's not a perfect analogy, it may trigger some interesting thoughts.

People ask, "How long can businesses continue to consolidate? When do the mergers stop? How high can the sand pile go?"

Conventional thinking is that mergers work when there are increased productivity efficiencies to be gained. This productivity is determined by the output divided by the number of human beings involved.

Of course, humans are involved, so the cultural aspects and social needs become important. Growth in the size of an organization is often at odds with these needs.

If companies can organize properly to satisfy the needs of the individuals, they can continue to merge. But simply building the pyramid higher results in operational inefficiencies, due to bureaucratic policies and systems that de-humanize the environment, and therefore, offset the advantage of economies of scale.

A band is a self-directed team. They determine their own success, rely on feedback from their audience and have different members leading at different times. Pictured here is one of The Phelps Group bands.

So How Does the Team Concept Work Best?

How can teams be fielded to deliver both the advantages of small teams and the power of a larger organization? Here are several key thoughts:

- Ensure that the individual, team and company or project goals are in alignment. This alignment is critical for maximum harmony and productivity.

The successive steps to ensure this are:

- Determine the individuals' short- and long-term objectives.
- Confirm that these objectives are aligned with the team's, and ultimately, the company's objectives.
- Confirm the members' commitments of deliverables over a specific time period.
- Determine how the individual will be measured and evaluated. Agree on how they will be compensated.
- Hold team members accountable to their goals and commitments. In this arrangement, it's not a matter of reward or punishment. It's a business agreement.
- Give team members freedom to operate as they see fit by minimizing the number of rules regarding how goals will be achieved.
- Agree that all team members will commit to gathering feedback for guidance.

To do this the organization must:

- Train the members to seek and accept feedback.
- Provide a full-feedback environment for their guidance. (This allows the individual and the team the freedom to get the job done when, where and how they believe it needs to be; use their problem-solving and entrepreneurial instincts; reap what they sow; and learn from their mistakes.)
- Solicit and listen to the team's input as to who is to be on their team.
- The company must provide the resources that the individuals and teams could not reasonably supply for themselves due to economies of scale:
  - ✓ Financial security should be spread over multiple clients/projects in the form of monetary income
  - ✓ Health insurance, etc. (Employment should not be a hand-to-mouth experience. Otherwise, why not just freelance?)
  - ✓ Sources of feedback for guidance (See Chapter Two, "Creating a Full Feedback Environment.")
  - ✓ Administrative support
  - ✓ Facilities and equipment
  - ✓ Financial support/systems for purchases on the customer's behalf
  - ✓ Company brand awareness, trust and customer loyalty

We encourage individual freedom.
We expect initiative.
We emphasize alignment in purpose.
We reward individual excellence.
We demand teamwork.

(a creed at The Phelps Group)

Give Them What They Want. (And Get What the Company Needs.)

We are adamant about self-directed, client-based teams because we believe that's the best way to give clients what they want!

Marketing, the essence of business, is simply the process of taking products or services to market. There are lots of textbook definitions of marketing. Here's our definition:

> *"Marketing is finding out what the customer wants and giving it to them."*

It's the same thing when it comes to getting the most out of a company's people. Just find out what they want and give it to them. (What people really want is listed a few pages back.) If a company hires people who are talented, experienced, self-motivated and aligned with the company's goals, then it simply becomes a matter of supporting those people with the resources they need in a healthy working environment.

It's Enlightened Self-Interest.

Building a strong entrepreneurial culture, where internal conflict is replaced with a sense of personal and corporate responsibility, will produce superior results.

So there's no justification for feeling overly virtuous or generous if you give your associates what they want. It's in *your* best interest. It's business. It's life in general. The more you give, the more you get. Help someone else, and help yourself. Be a friend, get a friend.

Give people what they feel they need to do a great job, and they'll give you their best effort.

Focus on the Customer – Not the Producer.

The optimum focus of organization for a business is the *customer* – not the company. And definitely not a department within a company!

The customer has the power, not the producing company. If there is consumer demand, someone will build, produce or make the product or service, demonstrating that the consumer truly has the power.

 Pyramids Are Tombs

Departments are dead.

They're buried in the Pyramids!

People Are Motivated by Their <u>Own</u> Goals.

The philosophy in top-down, pyramid-type organizations is that authority motivates people.

The philosophy of self-directed teams is that individuals and teams are motivated by their own goals and commitments. And when they're in alignment with the company and its clients, it's a win/win/win/win situation.

To achieve this, we organize around the client. Mental templates that help describe this are:

- There are *no* functional departments.
- The *entire* company is one department – the customer service department.
- Each client has its *own* department at the agency. But we eliminate the "D" word. We call these client-centered departments, *client-based, self-directed teams.*

Make It Faster, Better, Cheaper.
And By the Way, Integrate It, Too.

What does the customer invariably want? Faster, better and
cheaper, please!

In the past the demand for faster, better and cheaper was
answered, "Pick any two," inferring that it was only
possible to deliver any two of the three. In today's warp-
speed, technologically driven environment, two is simply
no longer good enough. Three isn't good enough either.
There's a fourth. As the world becomes more organized,
and the convergence of elements adds to the efficiencies of
systems, all the elements must be properly *integrated.*
Integrated – meaning aligned, in phase and working in a
synergistic way – so that the whole is greater than the
simple sum of the parts.

This means that service companies must *organize* to deliver
not only faster, not only better, and not only cheaper, but
in a more integrated fashion, too.

Eight Steps to Flattening a Pyramid.

Here are some changes that will create an organizational model for delivering faster, better, cheaper *and* integrated services:

1. Dismantle departments.
2. Re-organize in teams around the client with the specialists needed on the teams.
3. Move accountability from department heads to these client-based teams.
4. Move department heads to coaching positions. (Depending on your size, you may need to have "playing coaches," meaning they play on one team and coach the specialists in their discipline on other teams.)
5. Hold coaches responsible for the recruitment, inspiration and education of the specialists in their disciplines. Coaches consult, guide, inspire and encourage these specialists, but do *not* take on the final responsibility for the specialists' work. This accountability must remain with the individuals and within the client-based teams.
6. Install multiple mechanisms to give all individuals and teams liberal amounts of timely and constructive feedback from their peers, clients and suppliers on their work and interpersonal performance.

7. Eliminate conflicts of interest related to income for alignment of financial goals. (This is the Mother Lode! The answer to this one question should pay for this book 1000 times over. Read on.)
8. Promote an understanding that physical location and size of workstation do not relate to seniority or power.

Turf Wars: A No-Win Situation.

Imagine the heads of typical public relations, promotions and direct marketing departments or even worse, *divisions* of a large agency, paying a visit to one of their company's clients.

The client asks for their recommendations on how to solve a marketing problem. The head of the public relations department advises to move more money from the other areas into PR (because her compensation is directly related to the amount of billing that her department has). Not so surprisingly, for the same reason, the other department or division heads follow suit.

The result is what Don Schultz of Northwestern University calls a "silo mentality." The term aptly describes people working as if they're deep inside a silo, who can only see their own world, and who are oblivious to anything going on outside their own. A place where people are confused about, or distracted from, their intended role of giving clients the professional advice they're paying for. Departments in service organizations often create conflicts of interest between what the client wants and how something is done in a specific department or what a department wants to "sell."

The department develops ways that are most efficient for producing what they normally produce. Sometimes the client's special needs just get in the way. ("We don't do it like that in this department.") We've all been exposed to this attitude at different times in our lives. We invariably come away thinking, "Hey, who's the customer here, anyway?"

Departments often resist collaboration with other departments because they won't be compensated for the time they spend – since their compensation is dependant on the revenue that flows through their department.

Departments have department *directors* who are most often compensated by how much revenue flows through their department. This can be a financial incentive to put the department's needs ahead of the client's best interest. This conflict of interest can set up turf wars over how different departments want to carve up a client's budget.

Imagine an insurance agency where the life insurance department wants to maximize the client's expenditure for life insurance, while the property insurance department wants to maximize the client's expenditure for property insurance. Whose interest is at heart? The client's? Or the department's?

So, who's the client to believe? This is why so many clients eventually feel that they are being ill-served by their "professional" partners?

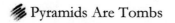

Departments are pyramids.

Pyramids are tombs in the communications age.

The Client Is God. (And So Are We.)

In most major religions, God is on the throne. As long as that priority is followed, everything flows smoothly from there.

Another way to view this – which is espoused by the major Eastern religions – is we are *all one*. This is especially true when the definition of an *agency* is considered.

An agency, by definition, is not a supplier to the client. It *represents* the client. It works on behalf of the client. It is, in effect, the client. Most professional service firms' long-term self-interest will be improved if they adopt this "agency" mindset.

We exist as one with the client. What is good for them is good for us – for we *are* them. We are their agency – not a supplier.

At The Phelps Group, we believe that what is truly good for the client, will, at least in the long term, be good for us. Any attempt to put the needs of our firm over those of the clients' is short-term thinking at the expense of our long-term success.

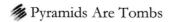

Have you ever been in a situation where you were caught
between the orders of your company's department head
and the client's needs? That conflict of interest most
often exists because of a flawed organizational model.

By demolishing functional departments, you help assure
that the client's needs are always on the throne. Then, no
one ever has to question who they work for. You know
you are working for the client.

Using The Phelps Group as an example of how this works:
There is no account management department and no
director of client services. So it's always crystal clear to
our team leaders and managers that they are working
directly for our clients. There is no media department,
and therefore no media director. Our media specialists
know that they work directly for the client (and client
team) they serve.

Our most experienced people with proven abilities to do
and teach – who would be department directors in other
organizations – are our *coaches*. When our specialists need
additional thinking from someone else in their discipline,
they're encouraged to seek it from whomever they wish,

and of course their coach is often their most qualified consultant.

But the coach doesn't mandate the answer. The specialists report directly to their team and their client(s). There's no doubt about for whom our specialists work.

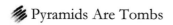

Gender, Age, Ethnicity and Geography Are Irretrievably Irrelevant.

A diverse workforce and open communications are hallmarks of many successful companies.

What we're advocating for service organizations – and proving in marketing communications – is the establishment of an environment of "self-directed teams nurtured by the resources of a mother ship."

In such an environment, the mix of gender, age, ethnicity and geographic location of the team members has evolved significantly from how teams would have been staffed just a few years ago.

Women are now more than one-third of America's workforce and increasingly better represented in the higher ranks – especially in the service sector.

More than 30% of the population in California is Hispanic. The majority of people in southern Florida were not born in this country.

Age is not the advantage it once was. In many industries today, especially those dominated by quickly changing technology – computers, software, telecommunications, etc. – the under-30 group, those born about the same time as the personal computer, often have better computer skills than their older associates.

We respect the wisdom that comes with age. But it's not about seniority.

It's not all about how hard we try either. We remind each other, "Let's not confuse effort with performance."

It's interesting to note that increasingly a team member's expertise is taking precedence over where the person is located physically. The practice of virtual teams using tele-conferencing, video-conferencing or web-conferencing is becoming commonplace. This also is true in the case of clients selecting professional service firms. What you know is more important than where you live.

The point here is simply that self-directed teams will increasingly be comprised of a more diverse workforce. These people will be more in tune with customers' needs as the marketplace becomes more global. And, due to vastly improved communications and transportation technologies, organizations will be decreasingly limited by their geographic location.

The Fast Eat the Slow in the Land of the Quick and the Dead.

In this age of quickly changing technology, it's no longer just the big eating the little. Now, in the land of the quick and the dead, the fast eat the slow.

Speed to market is critical.

Remember learning in school that business was all about land, labor and capital? Forget it. The new elements for business success are *technology, marketing* and *speed.*
Here are three qualifying questions to ask of yourself or your company:

1. Do you have a new technology that gives you a competitive edge for a window of time?
2. Do you know how to market it?
3. Can you get it to market fast – before someone else meets the consumer need you're filling?

Let's look at the third element of *speed* and how it relates to teams:

In most top-down hierarchies, in order to get something accomplished, a project must go "up the pyramid" for approval at each major stage.

As the project goes up through the layers of management for approval, each layer of management feels compelled to add its mandates and put its fingerprints somewhere. And as each change is mandated, the work comes back down for revisions before it can proceed to the next level.

Sometimes the piece being reviewed and approved is improved, but more often it's compromised by the "meddling and diddling" that occurs at each level. The higher you are on the pyramid, the further you are from the realities of the front lines. So your edits/changes are not necessarily improvements.

Front-line decision makers who deal with the suppliers and deliver the services to clients on a daily basis are often better informed than their CEO about such areas as the effects that disruptive technologies like the Internet and new software solutions can have on customer service. The actual architects of the project are often demoralized by the changes made to their work as it scales the pyramid. And projects are often slowed to the speed of a glacier!

The supervisors and the supervisors' supervisor are not usually at their desks waiting to review and approve. They're often unavailable at the time they're needed. So the project languishes. Pages fly off the calendar and the competition might win the game because of faster speed to market.

Self-directed teams are faster. Period.

These teams, working in a full-feedback environment, are able to draw on the seasoned experience of others in the organization for consulting and quality control, remain accountable for their own work and deliver the work on schedule.

Here's a little joke on this subject, sent to me by a friend:

It's called: *The Plan.*

> In the beginning was the plan.
> And then came the assumptions.
> And the assumptions were without form,
> and the plan was completely without substance.
> Darkness was on the face of the workers
> and they spoke to their supervisor, saying:
> "It is a crock of dung and it stinks."
>
> The supervisors went to their section managers and said:
> "It is full of dung and none may abide the odor thereof."
>
> The section managers went to their managers and said to them:
> "It is a container of excrement and it is very strong, such that none here may abide by it."
>
> The managers went to their general managers and said to them:
> "It contains that which aids plants in growth and is very strong."
>
> The general manager went to the vice president and said to him:
> "This powerful new plan will actively promote the growth and efficiency of the department, and this area in particular."
>
> The president looked upon the plan and saw that it was good.
>
> And it became policy.

Quality In/Quality Out.

You might ask, "If the teams aren't reporting to department heads, how do you control quality in a company of self-directed teams?"

You find the right people and allow their talents to breathe and grow in a healthy, *full-feedback* environment. They'll take it from there.

You'll read more about this in other parts of this book. However, just to cover the basics here:

Dr. W. Edward Deming, in his "Deming Method," advises putting the emphasis on the *first* part of your processes. We interpret that to mean screening, recruiting and properly deploying the right people.

For our purposes, we've determined that the next step is to create a full-feedback environment for all our people. If an individual or a team receives the proper feedback from the critical sources, they'll usually deliver the right answers. (You could blindfold someone, give them feedback about their movements and surroundings, and guide him or her down a busy street with little resistance.)

For this concept to work, team members must seek and receive honest, timely feedback from their team members, the team's peers in the company, the client, the client's customers and even suppliers. Life is a game of "pin the tail on the donkey." Just listen to the feedback and you'll reach the goal.

Everyone wants to succeed. People don't need rubber-stamped approval of their work. They need information to make it better. When they get it, they usually apply it. If they don't apply it, or apply it wrongly, they learn from their mistakes – or possibly even invent something new and better.

If It's So Great, Why Aren't More Companies Organized This Way?

It's interesting to note that Ed Deming had great success when he went to Japan and basically said, "Get rid of the quality control guy on the end of the line and make the team assembling the car responsible for its quality."

Then, as mentioned earlier, America's first "Deming car" was the Ford Taurus – which quickly became America's best-selling car.

That was the self-directed team concept at work in the rust belt! So why has it taken so long to catch on in the service industries?

It could be that Detroit had "bottomed out." Japan had brought them to their knees, so they were willing to make radical changes. Plus, Deming and the Japanese had already proved the concept in the auto industry.

The professional service industries may be clinging to the old ways because the movement of the economy, from being manufacturing-based to being service-based, has compensated for and covered up the inefficiencies of their outdated organizational models. The common reasons to resist change sound like: "What do you mean you're going to abolish my department!?", "If it worked before, it will work now." Or, "I don't want to rock the boat."

The need to change, and the opportunities for those who do, aren't as obvious as they were for Detroit's auto manufacturers, because strong demand for professional service people may partially cover up their organizational inefficiencies.

It's my belief that the competitive pressures created by those who do move to the more effective organizational model of fast-moving, self-directed teams will force the laggards to change.

Seven Compelling Reasons For a Company to Organize in Self-directed, Client-based Teams.

The self-directed team (working in a full-feedback environment) organizational model delivers:

1. *Competitive advantage when recruiting* quality personnel. (See earlier chapter, "A relentless search for ways to maximize human potential.")
2. *Improved associate retention* resulting from a more challenging and satisfying job.
3. *Enhanced client service* as a result of better communications with the client, which is the result of direct contact with the clients by more team members.
4. *Improved client retention* as a result of better service and multiple points of contact. This results in more individuals having relationships with more client contacts. Workers value client contact. It's a show of trust. Therefore, staff turnover is reduced when more people have client contact.
5. *Higher quality work* as a result of people feeling more responsible for their contribution to the work.
6. *Improved operations effectiveness and efficiencies* resulting from having fewer people "supervising" and more people actually doing the work. The conflict of interest of reporting simultaneously to a department head and the client has been removed, which eliminates "job security make-work" so common in multi-layered hierarchies. It also eliminates time delays created by too many internal approvals.
7. *Enabling of reasonable profits* as a result of the improved operational efficiencies and *all* the team members being responsible for the economic outcome for the agency and the client. This results in reduced write-offs due to better communication among the team members. Information theory says

that *every relay doubles the noise and cuts the message in half.* The objective then becomes to have the lowest number of layers to keep the organization as flat as possible.

Flattening an organization takes commitment and stamina.

The uncommitted need not apply.

And Yes, There's Pain Involved.

(For the short term anyway.)

It takes tremendous energy to fight the deep conditioning and inertia of the status quo. An organization shouldn't even consider trying this unless the CEO is totally committed to the concept and is willing to pay the price of the time and effort to make it happen.

Department or division managers surround CEOs. Department managers are the last to want their departments abolished. Often their self-image is based on how many people report to them.

The reorganization to self-directed, cross-functional teams will happen only when the CEO is totally committed to organizing *around* the client – and is willing to swim against the tide of department managers fighting to maintain their fiefdoms.

The first step is to have the coaches (former department heads) understand that they can have what they most likely really want in their jobs without having people report directly to them. Once the department managers begin performing as *coaches* and feel the relief of the responsibilities for the actual work shifting from their shoulders to the specialists doing the work, they're on their way to supporting the concept.

And once your coaching team is behind the concept, the pressure on the CEO is somewhat reduced and the support for the program is increased significantly.

What Happened to the "Ladder"?

Generations have grown up thinking in terms of "climbing the corporate ladder." This new organizational model throws the obsolete ladder away. And it takes awhile for some people to understand how advancement works in this new dynamic of self-directed teams.

It's sometimes scary to realize there's no "mommy or daddy" (department heads) to approve the work. (Father doesn't know best. The team does!)

It takes time for associates to realize that this model rewards their successes by giving them more direct client contact, more interesting projects, more internal recognition and increased compensation. Plus, it doesn't move them "up a ladder" into a position they may not be suited for.

Here's how it's worked in the advertising business for decades: A talented art director is rewarded for creating distinctive designs by being promoted to Creative Director. A creative director must manage people. Most art directors I know are not people leaders or managers. They are craftspeople. They are now miserable because they're doing too much of what they don't do well, and they're doing less of what they do well. That's a promotion?!

In the same spirit, great architects, lawyers and doctors may be better off focusing on their craft, rather than being "promoted" to manage other craftsmen. Promotions to management, as a result of being a good craftsman is often an excellent example of The Peter Principle: the effect of being promoted one level above your capabilities or interests.

Self-directed teams (operating in a full-feedback environment) eliminate this problem.

If You Disagree – Let's Hear Why.

The method for getting all associates to buy-in on the necessary operational and philosophical covenants starts during the hiring process and never really ends.

For example, at The Phelps Group, we require understanding and agreement on our "Covenants" which are:

> To reach our potentials, we must have alignment as to *what* we're doing, *where* we're going and *how* we're getting there. We are committed to the covenants below.

> If you disagree, let's hear why. You may have a good point. If so, we'll make adjustments.

> If you agree – great. Let's do it.

> Our **vision** is to be the standard by which all other marketing communications agencies are measured

> Our **mission** is to do great work for deserving clients, in a healthy working environment, to realize our clients' goals and our potentials.

> Our **core competency** is our ability to apply customer-focused integrated marketing disciplines in our clients' best interests.

Our work influences millions of people daily.
Therefore, truth is our *highest value* and our
guiding light.

We are *organized* in self-directed, client-based
teams of specialists, delivering IMC programs from
a full-feedback environment.

We are *accountable* for our work,
and we intend to deliver more than we promise.

Minimizing the Weaknesses.

Radical shifts in organizational structure will leave cracks in the wall that need attention. Here are some areas that require special attention when the structure changes from functional departments to multi-functional, self-directed teams:

Some people want to focus only on their area of expertise.

Sometimes team members feel they're spending too much time on matters other than their own craft. Sometimes they're right. This method of operation requires a strong *time management* discipline.

Some people need more direction than others.

At The Phelps Group we eschew job descriptions. Everything flows from the objectives and plans our teams write for their clients, for themselves as individuals and as teams. This eliminates our all-time least favorite comment, "That's not my job."

This can be an unsettling situation for people who are not accustomed to goal setting, plan writing or individual and team accountability. For example, account people who are simply "messengers" or "bag carriers," and writers who

have relied too much on the mystique of their eccentric personalities are exposed for their lack of contribution. Everyone stands naked (symbolically, obviously) in front of their team and the agency. There's no place to hide in an open, self-directed, performance-measured environment.

Some people are not good at client contact.
Some people are better than others at client contact. So there can be embarrassing moments.

But then again, let's not underestimate the clients' intelligence or their level of expectations.
Clients most often find it refreshing to talk directly to the craftspeople actually doing the work. For example, in marketing communications, those are the art directors, designers, writers, content developers, programmers and other craftspeople who are more focused on honing their craft than their human relations skills.

Vigilance is required.
So even though the advantages to self-directed teams are numerous, the organization must be on guard for the weaknesses pointed out here.

A Word About Financial Disclosure.

You can't expect teams to be self-directed if they're not privy to the account, team and agency profitability numbers. This is not a simple matter.

At The Phelps Group, we share all financial information except individual salary figures.

I wish I could say that our cost accounting systems, by account, give absolutely accurate pictures of the financial performance and productivity output at the individual, account and team levels. We're just not there yet. We're closer than we were a few years ago, but we have a long way to go. There's so much *intra*-team and *inter*-team support by individuals, it makes it nearly impossible to draw clear lines to determine exact contribution to income, expense and profit.

Increasingly sophisticated software and people's ability to use it will add clarity to this over time.

Redundancy Causes Inefficiencies – and Breakthroughs.

In order to integrate disciplines, it's imperative that people working on cross-functional teams understand some intricacies of other disciplines. Such issues are related to timing, cost, risk and the effort required.

Proper cross-training – so that the team members better understand the processes of the other specialists – takes time. The idea of multiple people dealing with the same issues is rife with redundancies. This can slow things down and add to time spent on a job for which a client doesn't want to pay. Significant problems can arise if time is mismanaged.

On the other hand, some of our freshest ideas come from the specialists who are not primarily responsible for a task. Much myopia and tunnel vision are eliminated when eyes from different disciplines look at a challenge. We've found that art directors can have bright ideas about financial matters. Media people edit headlines, etc. One of our first-year public relations specialists wanted to try his hand at advertising writing. He wrote a radio commercial for a national media buy that was chosen over the work of our most senior writers. And because his success was *their* success, they were happy see this young man's work chosen for production.

Big Payoffs Typically Require Big Investments.

We've invested many "man years" of time in developing our philosophies, covenants and systems. In our industry all we have to sell is our time – so this was a significant investment. It probably was more expensive for us than for agencies that follow us in adopting this method of organization. (Please, learn from us. The basics we learned from years of trial and error are right here in this book. Feel free to replicate the culture or processes in areas where you believe they will improve your organization.)

Then there's the cost of orienting and training *new* associates who come from top-down hierarchies, and the expense incurred when companies need to remodel their physical environments to accommodate the new working style.

We designed and built the interior of the The Phelps Group's building to reflect our working style. We have "The Ballroom" for our BrainBangers' Ball™, and "The Wall" to expose our work to feedback. (These mechanisms are explained in detail in later chapters.)

Since our beginning in 1981, we've had no individual offices. We cluster our open workstations in teams, not functional departments. Our PR people sit next to media, producers next to promotions people, etc. This accelerates learning about each other's disciplines and breaks down barriers to better communications.

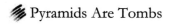

Self-directed, Client-based Teams, vs. Multi-layered Hierarchies.

So, yes, there are downsides to reorganizing to better serve the client: mental pain caused by resistance to change; and prices to pay in time and money.

Yet, we're passionate about this organizational concept at The Phelps Group.

The client-based team structure, when operating in the proper environment, provides natural alignment to fulfill the needs of the individual, the company, and the customers they serve. Everybody wins.

We're all mind workers. We like freedom. We realize the importance of speed. We trust each other to give constructive, timely criticism.

We think companies organized in this manner will attract the best people and enable these people to perform at their highest level. Plus, the customer will be heard and better served.

Ways to Flatten the Organization for Fun and Profit.

There are so many tell-tale signs of the old world that appear normal to some – because it's all they've ever known. When the structure changes, so must the cosmetics, because form usually follows function.

The physical layout, titles, dress codes, the common language used, how information flows, who talks first, and who critiques whom – these are the trappings that reflect the philosophy of a company.

Here are some of the cultural norms we have modified at The Phelps Group to bring these elements into alignment with our organization's working model.

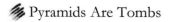

Change the language – and the behavior follows.
Our language is like a computer's operating system. We are programmed by it. Here are some words and phrases we do (and don't) encourage to effect a change in attitudes.

Don't use:

Boss – it's an old world word. Try team leader, manager, associate or whatever is appropriate. Individuals are their own boss. They don't even have to show up. They simply determine their own level of success by reaping the positive or negative consequences of their actions.

The more responsibility you have, the more you're actually working *for* the people around you. So say they work *with* you, not for you. And say you work *with* someone, not for them.

ASAP – busy schedules and relative importance of tasks render this acronym almost meaningless. Best to agree upon a specific date and time.

Departments – we abolished them at The Phelps Group and refer to people of the same skill as being in the same *discipline*.

Employees – it smacks of people working *for* others. *Associates* seems to work best for us.

Creatives – used in some ad agencies to refer to art directors and writers. This infers that our PR people aren't creative. Or our promotion people, or producers aren't creative. Or, anyone for that matter. It doesn't work in an IMC environment. We refer to our associates by their function: writer, PR specialist, producer, art director, etc.

Sold – don't use "we *sold* it to the client." Better to say, something like, "We *agreed* on the concept." The spirit being that we came to the same conclusions and have alignment on next steps. No one wants to be *sold*. If you don't have alignment, it won't stay sold for long.

I – when referring to what has been accomplished. Give the credit to the team when it's believable.

Tear down the walls.
Let the light in. Let communications flow freely. Encourage unexpected conversations. Encourage being out of your "office" and working with others.

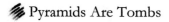

Abolish walled offices, which have traditionally been symbols of hierarchical rank.

Have everyone work in comfortable, functional, efficient work stations designed for people who spend most of their time on the computer or on the phone. Size these workstations so that they promote the use of common meeting rooms for groups larger than two or three (which tend to get loud).

Have the senior level associates "walk the talk" by having standard-sized workstations. Give the less experienced associates some of the larger workstations, to make it apparent that workstation size and location have nothing to do with a person's value to the company.

Let the savings from needing fewer square feet per person flow to lower prices to clients, higher salaries, retirement funds and higher profits.

Make titles functional – not hierarchical.
Avoid:
Supervisor – no one wants to be supervised. They want to be led. They want to be coached.

Executive – who *isn't* an executive in professional services in a flat organization? Words like specialists, managers, leaders may work better.

Senior – it's a relative term. Age is not much of an issue. Productivity is the yardstick, not seniority. And in many cases the younger are more productive because of their technological skills or energy level. This is not to say that we don't respect and revere the wisdom that comes with age and experience. But titles are not the place to show this respect. (Plus once you're over 40, you'd probably rather not be referred to as "senior.")

With this spirit in mind, consider allowing people to make up their own titles. The guideline is to be *descriptive* of the functions performed, not a person's relative importance within the organization.

In this same spirit, encourage the use of first names. Have the youngest people call the oldest by their first name. Publish phone lists alphabetized by first name. It's friendlier.

Speaking of lists: Always list people alphabetically – never by rank. This goes for lists of client names as well – even if the client organization still adheres to the old style in its own communications. Don't waste time and suffer anxiety figuring out a pecking order when building "To" and "CC" lists on a memo or report. People aren't offended by seeing their name in alpha order. (But they *are* offended if you happen to put them lower then they expect in a pecking order listing.)

Have fun!

> Our esprit de corps is the core of our success.
> It's the most difficult for a competitor to imitate.
>
> They can buy the physical things. The thing they can't buy is the dedication, devotion – the feeling we're participating in a cause or a crusade.
> *Herb Kelleher, former CEO, Southwest Airlines*

We all know it comes down to the people. Our belief is that happy people are more productive. And conversely, the people who are most productive are probably the happiest people.

So we work hard on the "wa" (Japanese term for harmony) at our agency. Our clients, suppliers and other visitors comment on it. They say they can feel it when they walk in the front door.

There is no one key to creating a fun atmosphere. But my sense is that it doesn't start with fun toys, colors or dogs. It starts with the vision and mission — and from that point, the rest is details.

Abolish rules for dress, attendance and work hours.

This is not as radical as it may sound.

The way we address these situations is to operate with the understanding that we hire only adults. Meaning, our associates must be smart and aware enough to:

- Know when their teammates need them to be in the office
- Know when and how to alert their teammates when they're not in the office
- Know which meetings to attend (once they've been notified a meeting is scheduled)
- Know how to dress to show an acceptable level of respect for their teammates and clients (after all, our company is in the business of building images)

Our associates' performance is measured by how well they meet their company-related goals by their contribution to:

- The quality of the work
- Our profit
- Our environment

Our associates are measured by their performance, not hours spent in the office. It's about productivity. As important as *effort* is, it may not equate to *performance.*

Working 50 hours a week doesn't necessarily make someone more valuable to the organization than someone who works 40 hours. If one believes they can increase their productivity 50% by working 60 hours. It's their life, and they'll reap the consequences – whether it's an increase in salary, the chance to work on more exciting client projects, a damaged home life or a one-dimensional life totally focused on work.

Ours is not piecework done on an assembly line. We virtually never produce something exactly the same way twice. Things change. We get better at what we're doing. Every job is a custom job. We're always *thinking.* Our clients pay us for our brand-building, sales-generating ideas. Who knows when these ideas may appear?

So considering the fact that we hire self-motivated, success-driven individuals who are working (thinking) when they are in the shower, at the breakfast table, on the freeway, while meditating, in the bar or on the golf course – not to mention 2 a.m. press checks, weekend trade shows and

16-hour film shoots – who are we to say when they must be in the office?

In fact, it's important to remind associates from time to time to be careful about judging others by when they happen to arrive at the office. Only that person knows what's going on in their life. And they are the one who reaps the reward (or lack thereof) for their level of work. The success of this way of working is affected by our associates' ability to be assertive enough to speak honestly to a teammate when that person's schedule is interfering with the team's productivity or work relationships.

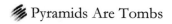

Knowledge Is Power – So Spread It Around.

Years ago I worked for a company that held "Creative Review Boards." As a more junior person, I didn't attend many of these meetings, which were populated by a lot of grey-haired people. I just knew that when these review boards were over, most of the people whose work was being reviewed were frustrated with the changes they were required to make to their work – and not many people outside that room learned *anything* from the meetings.

Contrast that situation with one where virtually everyone in the agency learns from the critiques given in the spirit of improving or confirming the work and delivered in a safe, open environment.

You'll read more about this in Part 2, "From a full-feedback environment." But to illustrate how we share knowledge, here's one example of how we review creative:

The Brainbangers' Ball : Once a week we bring in lunch and the entire agency joins in a brainstorming/focus group session. The team brings their work in progress to The Ball. They remind the entire agency of the target and the communications strategy. Then, they show the work and listen to and record the feedback. Everyone hears the more experienced expert opinions. And the more experienced hear opinions from both male and female, young and old, from various ethnicities and all our marcom disciplines.

They might hear a PR specialist warn that journalists will not be interested if this particular angle is used on a media relations pitch. They might hear an art director say something like, "To make the logo more important to the layout, you don't have to make it larger, you just need to leave more space around it." Or a copywriter might make something easier to read by suggesting that fewer words would allow a larger typeface. The entire agency might learn what works and what doesn't work in alliance marketing by helping to brainstorm partners for a cross-promotion for one of our clients. Or an interactive designer might learn – along with the entire agency – that a particular navigational design is not intuitive because many people in the room were confused by it.

Less experienced associates' self-esteem and confidence is often raised when they receive positive feedback on their ideas. Some people learn from others that some of their thinking is outdated.

The entire agency sees the inner workings of a client when its projects are brought to The Ball. So when that team needs to reach outside itself for help, the other associates are somewhat up-to-speed on the client and the project.

It's almost unbelievable. But the entire agency sees every project of any significance as it moves through the processes. Try that in a pyramid structure!

Massive amounts of information are exchanged in a short period of time. Client work is improved. Consumer research with a large *qualitative* sample base is completed in a matter of minutes. And *the learning curve is accelerated* for *virtually everyone* – especially the less experienced.

Impressive creative, research and educational power is generated by this sharing of knowledge.

This is a "creative review board" at its best!

Everyone Holds Everyone Responsible.

In traditional, pyramid-like structures, the people at the top hold the underlings responsible for their actions. In our more egalitarian model, it's a two-way street.

This is possible only when a company's philosophy is designed with the buy-in of the associates. This philosophy, in the form of its mission, vision, values, methods of operation and specific financial goals, must be published and reviewed regularly.

When this happens, everyone knows and has ownership in the guidelines that naturally flow from the commonly held philosophy.

Here are some examples of this mutual accountability.

The CEO is not always right.

As the CEO of The Phelps Group, I am usually involved in selecting and pursuing new accounts. As a company, we have committed to having only "deserving clients" on our roster. (Those whose products enrich the lives of those who buy them and those clients who treat their agency fairly.)

I'm sometimes tempted, for one reason or another, to take on a client who doesn't meet these requirements. Yet, because of our published and often reviewed covenants, our associates know our true, long-term plan, and feel free to "hold up the mirror" and voice disappointment that we're pursuing a particular client. Thank goodness they feel confident enough to be assertive. Otherwise, I would have led us down the wrong road more than once.

Bust the leaders.

All we really have to sell is the time we spend working for our clients. We've learned how expensive it is to waste time in unproductive meetings. And no one has the right to waste others' time. So we've committed to holding the people who call meetings to be accountable for the productivity of the meeting. This means, among other things:

- Preparing an agenda for the meeting (preferably sending it in advance so people can come prepared)
- Inviting only the people whose time is required in the meeting
- Dismissing and inviting people on an as-needed basis
- Encouraging the less assertive to contribute
- Confirming that actionable items are recorded
- Confirming that someone commits to delivering the next step by a specific date

As a group, we have agreed that anyone can "bust the leader" by challenging her/his judgment in calling a meeting that doesn't adhere to the guidelines mentioned above.

It's irrelevant as to who is doing the busting. The other people in the meeting are encouraged to support this person for caring enough and being assertive enough to help "train" us in good meeting management. It's of benefit to us all.

In other words, it's the *value of the idea* or assertion. It's not about rank.

The logic behind the spirit of this agreement is that once an organization has agreed on philosophies then we can let peer pressure take over. It's no longer about top down mandates and control.

Let the less experienced present.
The more often someone presents to a group, the more *comfortable* they become with public speaking.

Before people present to a group they prepare more thoroughly – and consequently *learn* more.

The combination of our associates being more comfortable in speaking to a group, with the knowledge acquired in the process, makes them more valuable to us and our clients.

Like trees, organizations are healthier when they grow from the bottom up.

This is only one point of the logic that justifies allowing the less experienced to take the lead.

Additional advantages are that more fresh ideas will present themselves. In general, younger people suffer less from rigidity of opinion. They're more often open to new ideas. They bring something surprising and often creative to a problem-solving or educational session.

It's human nature to want to take the lead and show the way to those with less experience. But almost invariably, when we give the baton to these people, they rise to the occasion and pleasantly surprise us.

It's worth mentioning that when someone is *listening*, they can reflect and think more expansively than when they're talking. So it makes sense to have the less experienced speak first. Their knowledge gaps will show up and can be addressed. (Or others will learn from their fresh approach.) The meeting leader, can sum up the thinking – if needed – and add whatever may be needed to complete the picture.

Top-down, command-and-control organizations crush the spirit
and decrease the effectiveness of the front-line people.

105

A self-directed, cross-functional, client-based team consists of whatever specialists are needed to develop and execute a program for their client.

106

An Office

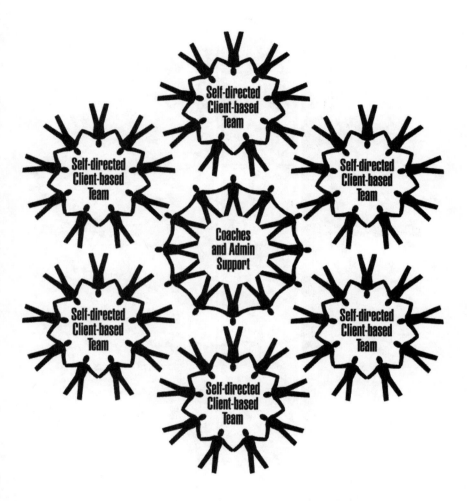

Self-directed teams are supported by administration and discipline coaches, who educate, advise and inspire, but who do not take responsibility for the work of those they coach. The responsibility resides with the team.

© The Phelps Group

Multiple Offices

The development of the structure is becoming obvious. The
geometry of the parts is repeated in the whole.

Holding Company

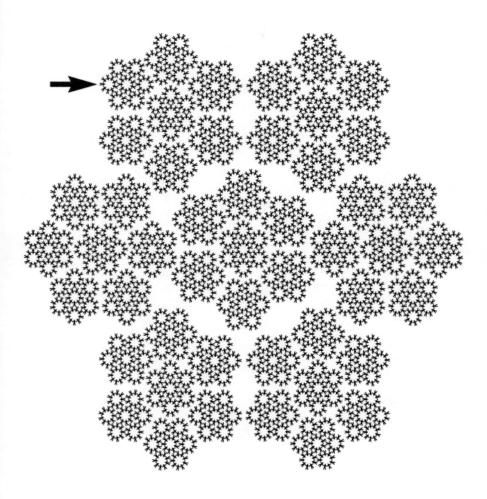

This illustrates the scalability of how the concept would work
for a holding company owning multiple agencies.

Part Two:
Creating a full-feedback
environment

Self-directed teams

Operating from a full-feedback environment

Creating a Full-Feedback Environment

Feeding Minds With Feedback.

The overall concept for the business model we're describing in this book is, "Find great people, bathe them in massive amounts of feedback about their work and performance – then get out of their way to let them get the job done."

They'll make the right decisions. If they don't, they – and the entire organization – can learn from their mistakes. The key is to institute this knowledge by having individuals report what they've learned to the group.

Feedback is the critical counterbalance to the autonomy enjoyed by self-directed teams. This chapter will explain in more detail the elements of the full-feedback environment as we've developed it at The Phelps Group.

There is a direct correlation between feedback and success. So, we want feedback from the same groups we depend on to help measure our movement toward our vision: our clients, our clients' customers, our peers, suppliers, community and ourselves.

The tools we use to gather this feedback include:

External:

- Client survey – of our performance by main client contacts.
- CEO-to-CEO conversations to review agency performance and clients' highest needs.
- Reports on client successes/failures due to our work.
- Supplier survey – of our performance by virtually all who send us invoices
- Family forum – we share our business plan with our families
- Outside classes – teaching and taking classes

Internal:

- 360-degree survey – annual critiques for individuals by their peers/teammates
- Group survey – critiques for the agency
- The Wall – written feedback on the work
- The WallBanger – weekly snacks at The Wall for verbal feedback on our work
- The Brainbanger's Ball – a focus group/brainstorming meeting on the work
- The eBanger – using email or the intranet to solicit ideas and feedback
- The EyeBall – face-to-face, 1-to-1 feedback on the work
- The PlayGround – occasional group creative sessions of art directors, writers and others
- Spring Advance – the agency working as one group off-site for two days to set goals and action plans

- Fall Retreat – off-site event where associates develop individual performance objectives for the year.
- Monthly 1-to-1s – feedback from coaches and team leaders on progress toward an individual's objectives.
- Monday Morning Meetings – to show finished work and deliver educational minutes.
- Safe environment – to encourage candid opinions at any time.

Client Surveys.

We've conducted in-depth client surveys every year since 1985. Clients are asked to evaluate how well we meet our commitments, how well we communicate with them and whether or not they feel we are providing quality service overall. The teams follow up to ensure the client knows we've heard their concerns and create action plans to make the necessary course corrections.

It's human nature to avoid uncomfortable conversations. So, if we don't receive a completed survey from a client, I follow up on the survey personally to get a report.

Here are the questions we ask in the client surveys. Each question can be checked as Strongly disagree, Somewhat disagree, Somewhat agree or Strongly agree. Below each question is a "Comments" space for additional input.

- You are thorough in your approach to your work.
- You show creativity in your proposed solutions.
- You return my phone calls and e-mails promptly.
- You are courteous.
- You keep your promises on deadlines.
- You do not waste our time.
- You offer fast turnaround when requested.
- You relate well to our people.

- You keep us sufficiently informed on progress.
- You notify us promptly of changes in scope of work and seek our approval.
- You don't wait for us to initiate; you anticipate.
- You have a good understanding of our business.
- You make us feel that we are important.

The following open-ended questions ask for comments:

- Are there any individuals who are providing exceptional service? (comments only)
- Are there any individuals who are providing less than satisfactory service? (Please note if you would prefer your answer to remain confidential)
- Are there any other comments about our agency you would like to share?
- Please fill in your name and company.

Supplier Surveys.

We ask our supplier/partners to complete annual surveys on our performance. This is a bit trickier, because the ones who may be the least pleased with us may not bother to return our questionnaire. A media rep or print supplier, may, for example, feel that if they criticize us for some reason that their contact at the agency may find another supplier. To correct for this, I follow up verbally and probe our important suppliers who do not return the survey.

We value positive, long-term relationships with key suppliers. They see us relative to their other customers. And they have a broader perspective in many ways, so their opinions obviously are very important.

Our suppliers want us to succeed. So we believe they should have solid understanding of our mission, vision and processes. Therefore, we hold an annual Supplier Dinner where we review our general business plan and ask for their ideas and opinions as to how we can improve as an agency.

For example, we learned at a recent Supplier Dinner that we weren't sending our agency newsletter, Creative Strategies, to our supplier partners. They also enjoy helping us by alerting us to opportunities where other agencies are finding success.

Below is a sample supplier survey.

1. To what extent are you aware of The Phelps Group's mission – the agency's overall purpose and reason for being?

☐ To a very great extent
☐ To a great extent
☐ To some extent
☐ To a little extent
☐ To a very little extent

2. How would you describe the accessibility of your contact(s)?

☐ Very accessible
☐ Somewhat accessible
☐ Average
☐ Not very accessible
☐ Not at all accessible

3. Do you feel that you're dealt with fairly (compared to your competition or relative to other agencies)?

☐ Extremely fairly
☐ Very fairly
☐ Somewhat fairly
☐ Not very fairly
☐ Not at all fairly

4. Are you given a proper chance to present your products/services?

☐ Always
☐ Most of the time
☐ Some of the time
☐ Seldom
☐ Never

5. How would you rate us in terms of financial dealings?
- ☐   Extremely favorably
- ☐   Very favorably
- ☐   Somewhat favorably
- ☐   Not very favorably
- ☐   Not at all favorably

6. How would you rate our performance in paying on time?
- ☐   Extremely favorably
- ☐   Very favorably
- ☐   Somewhat favorably
- ☐   Not very favorably
- ☐   Not at all favorably

7. How would you rate our office environment in terms of attractiveness?
- ☐   Extremely attractive
- ☐   Very attractive
- ☐   Somewhat attractive
- ☐   Not very attractive
- ☐   Not at all attractive

8. How would you rate our voice-mail phone system?
- ☐   Extremely favorably
- ☐   Very favorably
- ☐   Somewhat favorably
- ☐   Not very favorably
- ☐   Not at all favorably

9. How would you rate our receptionist, in terms of helpfulness and courteousness?
- ☐   Extremely helpful/courteous
- ☐   Very helpful/courteous
- ☐   Somewhat helpful/courteous
- ☐   Not very helpful/courteous
- ☐   Not at all helpful/courteous

10. In general, how competent do you believe group members are in their positions? *(Please leave blank if you are unsure.)*

	Extremely	Very	Somewhat	Not very	Not at all
Account Mgmt.	☐	☐	☐	☐	☐
Creative	☐	☐	☐	☐	☐
Media	☐	☐	☐	☐	☐
Production	☐	☐	☐	☐	☐
Public Relations	☐	☐	☐	☐	☐
Direct	☐	☐	☐	☐	☐
Promotions	☐	☐	☐	☐	☐
Interactive	☐	☐	☐	☐	☐

11. Do you feel that members of The Phelps Group communicate freely, openly and honestly with you?

☐ Yes
☐ No
☐ Uncertain

12. Overall, how would you rate the agency's account management services?

☐ Extremely well
☐ Very well
☐ Average
☐ Very poorly
☐ Extremely poorly
☐ Uncertain

13. Overall, how would you rate the agency's creative product?

☐ Extremely well
☐ Very well
☐ Average
☐ Very poorly
☐ Extremely poorly
☐ Uncertain

14. Overall, how would you rate the agency's media planning and buying services?

- ☐   Extremely well
- ☐   Very well
- ☐   Average
- ☐   Very poorly
- ☐   Extremely poorly
- ☐   Uncertain

15. Overall, how would you rate the agency's print production services?

- ☐   Extremely well
- ☐   Very well
- ☐   Average
- ☐   Very poorly
- ☐   Extremely poorly
- ☐   Uncertain

16. Overall, how would you rate the agency's broadcast production services?

- ☐   Extremely well
- ☐   Very well
- ☐   Average
- ☐   Very poorly
- ☐   Extremely poorly
- ☐   Uncertain

17. In general, how would you rate the agency's public relations services?

- ☐   Extremely well
- ☐   Very well
- ☐   Average
- ☐   Very poorly
- ☐   Extremely poorly
- ☐   Uncertain

18. Overall, how would you rate the agency's direct mail services?

- ☐ Extremely well
- ☐ Very well
- ☐ Average
- ☐ Very poorly
- ☐ Extremely poorly
- ☐ Uncertain

19. Overall, how would you rate the agency's promotions services?

- ☐ Extremely well
- ☐ Very well
- ☐ Average
- ☐ Very poorly
- ☐ Extremely poorly
- ☐ Uncertain

20. Overall, how would you rate the agency's interactive services?

- ☐ Extremely well
- ☐ Very well
- ☐ Average
- ☐ Very poorly
- ☐ Extremely poorly
- ☐ Uncertain

21. Overall, how would you rate the agency's accounting department?

- ☐ Extremely well
- ☐ Very well
- ☐ Average
- ☐ Very poorly
- ☐ Extremely poorly
- ☐ Uncertain

22. Overall, how do you perceive The Phelps Group's relationships with its clients?

☐   Extremely good relationships
☐   Very good relationships
☐   Average relationships
☐   Very poor relationships
☐   Extremely poor relationships

23. How would you rate The Phelps Group's newsletter *Creative Strategies*?

☐   Excellent
☐   Good
☐   Fair
☐   Poor
☐   I have not received *Creative Strategies*
☐   I would like to have my name added to your mailing list to receive *Creative Strategies*

24. How likely would you be to refer us to a company who is looking for a communications agency?

☐   Extremely likely
☐   Very likely
☐   Somewhat likely
☐   Not very likely
☐   Not at all likely

360-degree Surveys.

We conduct in-depth 360-degree surveys in which our associates evaluate their team members. Each associate has the benefit of knowing, on an annual basis, how at least seven of their peers, with whom they work on a daily basis, view their contributions to the team and to the agency. It allows associates to confront common criticisms or concerns about their performance that others seem to share.

As a group, we've learned how to get more out of these surveys. In the beginning, review comments were written as if the writer was complaining to "management" about the other person's performance. As a group, we agreed that it's best to write as if you are speaking directly to that person, and assuming that the recipient has good intentions, believes they're making a good effort and wants the best for the agency.

This has improved the spirit of the survey and the return on our investment of time.

Group Surveys.

We survey ourselves as an agency annually. We measure our progress against our mission and vision. Areas of performance covered include: agency planning, goals, measurement, education, communications, environment, facilities and equipment. We ask for ideas in general about how we can improve our processes and work for our clients.

Family Forum.

We have an annual "Mate-Night Dinner" at the agency. (No, not mating night!) We use this time to explain our mission, vision and progress to the most important people in our associates' lives. It's all part of our push toward total alignment. If the people we live with know what we're doing, they can help us with ideas, introductions and encouragement. They are more likely to have patience with us when we have to work an evening or a weekend, because they better understand why we're willing to invest the time.

Internal Feedback On Our Work.

We have three mechanisms for gathering internal feedback on our work as it's in progress: *The Wall*™, *The BrainBangers' Ball*™ and *The EyeBall*™.

The thinking behind these devices is that the client and the team make the decision on the work. The cultural element that adds creative power and security to this model is an understanding that all work will be subjected to the opinions and feedback from the entire agency. We call it "putting more brains on the work." It begins with commitments from the associates when they join our group that they will expose their work as it moves through its stages of development. It's enforced by peer pressure. After all, our work is shown to thousands and often millions of people. Why take the unnecessary risk of not getting the opinions of your associates?

Some of the factors that led to the development of these feedback devices are:

The speed at which jobs are produced nowadays often doesn't allow for copy testing. This increases the risk that the intended message may not be the message received or remembered.

The cost of a mistake can be crippling considering the large number of people who see our work and can be affected by it, and the cost of the media required to reach them.

We're capitalizing on the chance to improve the work by getting more minds on it – more ideas, more proofing.

People working day-to-day on an account can develop personal and team tunnel-vision. Fresh thinking from outside sources helps eliminate this problem.

Once again our basic philosophy is reinforced: Find great people, bathe them in feedback and get out of their way as they make the decisions they're best equipped and prepared to make.

The Wall™.

The Wall is our town square. We think of the hallway in front of it as a gauntlet. Webster defines a gauntlet as:

1. two lines of men facing each other, armed with sticks or other weapons with which they beat a person forced to run between them.
2. a severe trial or ordeal.

Although we don't beat on people, or hold severe trials at The Phelps Group, we've created The Wall, which serves as a 10-hour-a-day, 5-day-a-week feedback mechanism for work in progress.

The philosophy behind The Wall within our full-feedback environment is based on leaving the final decision to the team, but with the understanding that the "gauntlet has to be run." In other words, it means that at every stage of a project, the work must be shown on the wall to dozens of people acting as the target audience, armed not with clubs but with pens and pencils with which to offer a comment, praise, criticism or suggestion.

To illustrate how The Wall works: In our industry, a writer with a Clio award is considered successful. Well, Howie Cohen is in the Clio *Hall of Fame* twice, and has one of America's Top 5 best remembered campaigns ("I can't believe I ate the whole thing." For Alka Seltzer). When Howie first came to our agency as our Chief Creative Officer, after we acquired Cohen/Johnson, he already had bought in to our general concept. But he hadn't grasped some of its nuances.

One day he and I were looking at a comment on one of his ads for our shampoo client, Citre Shine. One of our female PR specialists, not long out of college, had written her critique of his ad on the layout. Howie said to me, "You mean I have to listen to a 23-year-old PR girl's critique of my ad?" I said to Howie, (who was in his 50s) "Howie, first of all she's a woman, and that's an ad for a product that a woman is most likely to buy. Second, she's in the age group most likely to buy it. And third, it's just information. You do what you want with it."

I could just see the light go on for Howie. We laughed. And Howie has been our most staunch supporter of The Wall over the past years.

The message any team sends when they take work out of the agency without probing for feedback is a very cavalier one. It might read like, "We're so good, we don't need the opinions of others who are not as close to this project as we are." Or, "We'd bet our jobs there are no typos in the work." Or, "Of course it's a great layout. I know my area. I did my best and I don't need others' opinions." Or, "I wrote it, so it is clear as a bell."

The Wall, a feedback mechanism for
The Work, invites additional ideas and
critiques, provides insurance against
errors and is a teaching tool for all levels
of experience.

It's the team's responsibility to keep the work exposed to the agency for feedback. And our training for team leaders is to communicate this logic:

Writers and art directors – and most people in our agency –
are trying to reach perfection. That's what makes them tick
and makes them great. They naturally will be reluctant to
turn loose of their project "babies" until they feel they're
complete. Problem is, by the time they're "complete,"
it's time to take them to the client. And that's too late
for feedback.

Here's the scenario we promote:

The objective and strategy of the project goes up on the
wall in simplified form for feedback when a project is
begun. The initial creative thinking goes up immediately.
The earlier we can get others' opinions on the work, the
better. Then the work proceeds as normal, while the teams
watch for valuable feedback.

Then, throughout the next stage (a tight layout, a press
release, a storyboard, etc.), the same process is repeated.
As the work moves through the production stages, the old
work is taken down quickly to eliminate time wasted by
critiquing ideas that are dead.

While this is happening, the energy level in the gauntlet is
high. People are taking things there and critiquing others

work while they're there. The better we get at it, the more we learn to separate the work from our personal feelings and the more often we turn good work into great work.

In normal pyramid situations, some people see some of the work as it moves through the processes. At The Wall, everyone sees virtually every significant project as it progresses. It's fun for the group, because everyone gets a chance to see what's in production and voice their opinion.

And it is just that – an opinion. We just consider it information. Because the team ultimately makes the decision about what goes to the client for consideration.

New associates are typically more protective of their work, and more sensitive to the public critiques. However, once they realize that it's all just information, and that final decisions are made by their client-based team, and that their success is dependant on how well the work performs – not how well it plays internally – they become more open to posting their unfinished work on The Wall.

Another advantage of The Wall is that it helps us to integrate campaigns. An ad concept may spark a media relations idea or an idea for a promotion.

It's valuable to write a signed comment on someone's work. Yet, it's more educational when people actually discuss the work face to face. Ideas spark other ideas. People learn about the accounts and the work. That's why we invented The WallBanger ™.

The WallBanger is held at 3 P.M. on the days we don't have lunch together. Around that time people tend to find some sort of a snack. So we provide healthy snacks at The Wall and our receptionist announces "The snacks are out and place to be is at The Wall."

When you want to get people together, just supply food. It works. We have serious conversations about the work, and just as often there's laughing and giggling – which leads to good ideas, too – and a welcome afternoon break from routine.

The BrainBangers' Ball™.

With technology making it possible to work from virtually anywhere, and with e-mail and voicemail taking the place of many conversations around the office, we feel it's important to create opportunities for all associates to come together on a regular basis. The weekly BrainBangers' Ball (BBB) serves two purposes. It gets us all together every Thursday for lunch to create much-needed face-time, and it allows for more feedback on our work during the critical stages of development.

At The BBB, team leaders, art directors, PR, direct, promotions and interactive specialists – anyone needing feedback on a project – all have a chance to tell the entire agency what their objective is, who the intended audience is, and then present their ideas in various stages of development. It might have to do with a broadcast or print ad, a PR campaign, a Web page or interactive contest, a promotion, or a direct response offer.

During The BBB – which has a tendency to be wild and wacky – the agency operates as a large, diversified focus group, and a brainstorming group. This results in simultaneous research and creation.

We devote 45 minutes to anywhere from two to six projects, with the entire agency focusing on the task. We call this having "more brains on our clients' business." This ethnically diverse, built-in focus group ranges in age from 22 to 65, represents both genders and is capable of generating a lot of feedback in a short time.

A member of the team presenting the work acts as a scribe to capture the feedback on a large projection screen. That way all associates can see that their ideas were recorded as they intended them. The teams are asked to consider all the input – without any obligation to use any of it. *It's up to the self-directed teams to accept or reject the information* they receive. This lessens the risk of decision by committee, which can compromise an idea or execution.

The BBB is an excellent tool for ranking preferences for concepts, brainstorming new product names, building lists of alliance partners and gathering additional ideas and opinions on virtually any type of work in progress.

When asking the group to critique, we suggest associates ask, "What could make this communication clearer?" Or, "If you were our target, would this inspire you to want to know more or to take action?"

Over time, the BBB has challenged us creatively, to nurture and develop the talents of less experienced associates, and to enhance the work. The value of the BBB far exceeds the agency's investment of time and money in it. In terms of benefit to our clients, it is some of the best unbilled (free) advice they'll ever receive.

Clients have been so taken by the concept that they occasionally attend our Thursday BBB. We enjoy the interaction with them in that setting. And they love seeing virtually every brain in the agency focused on their projects. In one memorable BBB, the Teradyne team was narrowing down the choices for a logo we designed for a new product line. The client and the art director favored one execution. When it came up on the screen, someone said, "It looks like a horse's ass going over a fence." After that comment, that's all anyone could see when they saw that logo.

It's fortunate that one of our associates saw it before it was produced. Because Teradyne's competitors would have had a field day with that one!

If something is chauvinistic, condescending or off-color, someone will point it out. Often better ideas come forth from the group than those being presented. Many ideas enhance the work, and even if that doesn't happen, the team gets confirmation that they're on the right track.

All in all, our BrainBangers' Ball is a worthwhile event. It's great for generating ideas. It provides "disaster check" research on the fly. It facilitates integration of the campaigns. The associates get to know each other's personalities and talents. And it's fun!

The BrainBangers' Ball serves as a focus group, a brainstorming session, and gets us together for food and face time.

The EyeBall™.

Too often, large amounts of time are spent by people polishing ideas for presentation in order to get internal buy-in. They may tightly edit copy or spend hours on a computer selecting colors and kerning typography. This can result in a waste of time and unnecessary frustration on the part of the specialists, because they've fallen in love with their concept, only to find later that the *concept* is weak.

For this reason we encourage participation in The EyeBall.

The concept of The EyeBall is to get our embryonic concepts exposed for any or all of the following reasons:

- when there's no time for The BBB or The Wall.
- to get feedback from the coaches.
- to get feedback from team members.
- to spur additional suggestions for solutions.

The self-directed teams make the decisions as to what goes to the client. So there's really no need to sell an idea to agency management. The team is better off getting critiques and response to their conceptual ideas. So, when that time is spent refining a concept, it has a better chance of actually hitting the page or the screen.

Associates are encouraged to make photocopies and to leave the copies on various people's chairs and ask them to react. Some associates have made excellent use of e-mail and Web-based surveys (such as Zoomerang) for quick polling and brainstorming.

PR specialists rely on The EyeBall for much of their writing. When responding to journalists leads, they're often on tight deadlines. So it's faster to run a pitch angle by a colleague.

The EyeBall also is an excellent educational tool. Associates reviewing work with their coaches learn from these more experienced people while they improve the quality of their concepts.

The PlayGround™.

The concept for this group creative session was born out of The BrainBangers' Ball. The thought was, "If we can get this kind of power from a 10-minute, all-hands brainstorming session in the BBB, what would happen if we focused a room full of our art directors and copywriters on a creative challenge?"

When we put this many brains on an issue, we like to get to the heart of the matter very quickly. So, The PlayGround process starts when the team responsible for the work has developed our Creative Roadmap which says:

If the target currently believes X

And we want them to believe Y

What do we tell them to change their belief?

Kent Land, art director and the associate who conceived The PlayGround, describes how it works:

> "I think the 'Sweet' ad we did for Roland would illustrate the benefit of The PlayGround: After the initial strategy was e-mailed, we met for about an hour to generate ideas and review ideas that people brought. The candy bar idea came while we were together from discussions about 'all the good things packed into this keyboard, and the headline,

142

'Sweet,' followed immediately as a simple hammer to drive home the promise.

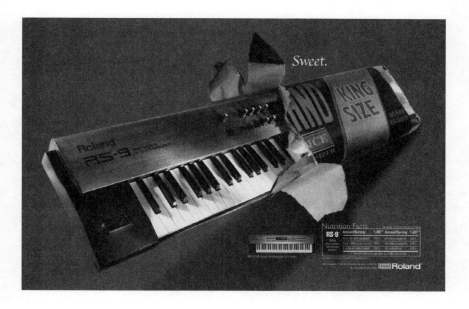

I believe there are benefits of more interaction between art directors and copywriters in The PlayGround, and it adds a great deal to the camaraderie and cooperation among those specialists. That's important within our structure because it offsets some of the isolation of the discrete team approach. It provides a forum that gets more eyeballs on the work – since we don't have an official creative director. It can help junior level people feel less pressure because The PlayGround offers a more level playing field and keeps any one person from dominating."

What is to be gained from The PlayGround?

- More brains on more work.
- More ideas.
- Better results.
- More knowledge of what everyone is doing.
- Creative ideas are allowed to come to life.
- More freedom/risk-taking for more breakthrough ideas.
- More face-to-face contact for better cooperation/inspiration.
- Shared responsibility for all the work from our agency.
- More ownership for more involvement.

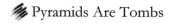

Education Is to the Information Age What Machines Were to the Industrial Age.

We tap our internal resources as well as outside speakers and educational institutions to constantly improve our knowledge base. Here are some of our educational mechanisms:

Monday Morning Meetings (MMM)

An important feedback and educational tool for us is our Monday Morning Meeting (MMM) at 9 A.M. We ask associates to plan their schedules to be in attendance. The meeting lasts between 30 and 60 minutes. We think a great way to start the week is to spend time with each other in a group setting. We are reminded that there are others we can rely on, others who care for us and who want to see us succeed.

A typical MMM will include client news, overall agency updates and discipline cross-training *"Minutes,"* when associates share information on their disciplines with others who are less familiar with their area of expertise. This way, for example, PR people can better understand the challenges facing media planners; art directors can learn more about how databases accurately "profile" target audiences, and copywriters can learn about new Internet

145

tools and techniques. Over a year, each discipline has the chance to share about 45 "Minutes" with our colleagues. This raises the entire agency's knowledge and expertise.

We may not learn other disciplines to the level of the specialists in those areas. But this helps us understand their processes. (It's harder to lead, manage or coordinate with processes you don't understand!)

Someone outside our agency, upon hearing about our *Minutes*, remarked, "Isn't it just like people in your industry to boil things down to a minute?" Exactly!

At each MMM, the "Way to Go" award for the week is given to a deserving associate in front of the entire agency. A brief explanation of why the person is receiving the award is given. The person is selected by the previous week's "Way to Go," winner and the award book is kept at the new recipient's workstation for that week. The giver of the award adds a page to the award book as a tribute to the person receiving the award. The recipient also enjoys use of the agency's only assigned (and prime) parking space for that week.

Monday Lunch Seminars.

The Monday Morning Meetings provide a solid start for the week. Then, at noon, further training occurs at the agency when we hold 45-minute seminars. As with The BrainBangers' Ball, the Monday Seminars are conducted after a catered lunch.

These seminars are balanced in number throughout the year in three categories:

Cross training: Our associates prepare seminar presentations, or we bring in outside experts who advance our understanding of each of our disciplines plus subjects like business law and new technological developments.

Life training: Outside experts and associates volunteer to cover issues such as personal health, time management, better communications, conflict resolution and safety issues.

Deep training: These are "breakout sessions" where the individual disciplines get together for more in-depth sessions. For example, the art directors get together to teach each other how to better use a particular software package. Or, PR specialists trade best practices on how to get journalists' attention.

Outside education: We want to be careful not to become insular in our thinking. So, we encourage (and pay for) our associates to continue their education through college programs, trade association seminars, workshops and membership in appropriate organizations.

If someone is willing to spend their evenings or weekends in class, we're happy to pay for it.

The race goes to the swiftest. To be the swiftest, you've got to be the *smartest*.

Is This Model Scalable?

The premise of this book is that self-directed teams organized around their clients is the most effective and efficient model for professional service companies. And that professional service companies organized by internal functions will become dinosaurs because they simply won't be able to react fast enough and in the best interests of their clients to be competitive.

It's my belief that the first two sections of this book covering self-directed teams, nourished by a full-feedback environment, are useful in helping a service company organize for the ultimate benefit of their stakeholders.

I've been asked if this concept is scalable? In years past, I've heard comments like, "Sure, Joe, this works for a company of 20 people, but will it work when you're larger?" The same question was asked when there were 40 of us. We now have more than 60 full-time associates, and although it's being asked less frequently, it bears discussion.

In regards to this subject, a memorable moment for me was at one of our yearly Spring Advances, in Warner Springs, California. We were in team breakouts. Four or five teams were spread out on a lawn working on their plans. Someone asked me how many teams I thought this model would handle. I told them I could see dozens of teams disappearing over the top of the hill.

Self-directed teams bathed in feedback may be more scalable – and extendable – than any organizational model to date for professional service companies.

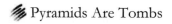

It's Scalable Because More Contacts Build Stronger Relationships.

Fact: Additional points of contact between the agency and the client can increase operational efficiencies and add to the stability of the relationship.

To illustrate: A few years ago, one of my mentors in this industry told me that few agencies ever get more than a dozen significant clients under one roof. This man led the growth of an agency from less than $250 thousand to more than $400 million. So, I always listened carefully when he spoke.

He said that there are only so many evenings in a month to spend at dinners and events with the clients' top management. It was those relationships that kept the client/agency relationship on track. And that when the agency roster got too large, some clients didn't get the attention from top management they required and would leave.

His agency, built in a pyramid-type, top-down, command-and-control model — like the others in the industry — had another problem. The account executives and supervisors were, in many instances, the only people who had client contact. So the client/agency relationship had very few contact points and much of the responsibility for relationship building was left to agency top management and account management. Since account management spent considerable time carrying routine tidbits of information back and forth between agency specialists and the client, strategic planning and production facilitation – often the most important aspects of their job – took a back seat to administration.

Contrast this with a client-based team:

- The client is resident on the team, and therefore welcomed and encouraged to speak to any team member.
- Multiple relationships are built.
- Team members, who in the old world didn't really work directly with the client, are now closer to the customer – and learn more by getting input directly from the horse's mouth.
- All information is not filtered through account management.
- Because the communication task is shared among team members, account managers and leaders spend more time on what the client actually wants from the agency.

On a related subject, it's this economy of time that allows an IMC team leader to facilitate multiple services – as opposed to facilitating only one discipline like advertising or PR or promotions, if they were at a single-discipline agency.

Take, for example, a client who wants to know the price of an insertion in a particular magazine. Contrast these two scenarios:

1. Example of a traditional pyramid-type structure, where the account executive is the client/agency liaison on almost all communications:

- Client calls the AE and asks for information.
- AE records the request and goes to the media department.
- AE gives the media specialist the request.
- Media specialist looks up the answer (while the AE waits).
- AE takes the information back to their desk, calls the client and delivers the information.
- If the answer sparks another question from the client, well – here we go again.

2. Example of self-directed teams where the client is on the team:

- Client calls the media specialist and asks for the information.
- Media specialist delivers the answer.
- If the client wants more information, they're already speaking to the specialist.
- Media specialist alerts account management of the communication.

(This last step is necessary when any team member works directly with a client, because we've agreed that account management needs to be current on all significant account activities.)

In the second scenario:

- AE's time is spent more efficiently.
- Media person benefits from the client contact.
- Client gets quicker and often more thorough service.
- Client sees how knowledgeable their media specialist is.
- Relationships are built with more team members.

This is just one example of where a routine task, handled by a client-based team, works to build knowledge and relationships.

Think about it: Workers (team members) talking directly to the market (the client) without going through management. There's something very refreshing – very honest about that, isn't there?

It does give rise to the need to "train" clients who are used to going thru one person that there may be a better way to do it.

(Sidebar: This is something that will increasingly happen in large business-to-consumer buying groups with the rise of Internet usage.)

The benefits of this model are:

- It builds deeper understanding among those actually providing and receiving the service throughout the organizations.
- It's genuine, because the responsibility for maintaining the relationship is shifted more to those actually working together on a daily basis.
- It allows more clients to be added to the roster without overburdening agency top management's workload.
- Because of the multiple relationships, the agency is less likely to lose an account if a key team member leaves the agency. This reduces turnover and improves client service.

It's Scalable Because Individual Freedom and Trust Are Maintained.

Fact: Pyramid-type professional service firms lose efficiency with growth.

Top-down, command-and-control models use policies to control individual action. They assume that management can write policy and workers will know and adhere to all policy. They condition their employees to be subservient executers of work orders handed down the pyramid, and they most often do not empower them to make decisions that they're most capable of making because of their hands-on experience.

Today's quick-change environment requires flexibility of policy to give the customer what they need at the moment, and allows neither the time to write policy for every situation nor the time required to understand and adhere to micro-management.

Conversely, the *teams bathed in feedback* model assumes that smart people who are committed to the philosophy of self-management and to exposing their work-in-progress to feedback will make the right decisions and don't need policy manuals.

Think about this in relation to the Enron/Anderson
debacle. If the employees at Anderson had been properly
sharing the power, would they have blindly obeyed orders
from above to shred documents?

It's Scalable Because Alignment and Accountability Are Not Compromised by Growth.

Fact: Uneven growth of departments can result in power shifts within an organization that color the service offering to the client. For example, in a traditional pyramid structure, if one department grows significantly stronger than another, it could influence the mix of services recommended to a client and create programs that are not aligned with the client's best interest.

Conversely, growth in the number of teams does not compromise alignment within self-directed, discipline-neutral, client-based teams.

Fact: Departments have department directors and these directors have the ultimate responsibility for all work performed within their department. That means the individuals performing the work do *not* have the ultimate responsibility for the work. The larger the organization, the more confusing it gets.

Conversely, in self-directed teams, there's never any doubt about who is responsible and accountable for the work. Therefore, accountability to individual goals is not compromised by growth in the number of self-directed teams in a company.

Combine this with the fact that more direct individual responsibility results in more personal satisfaction. Add to this the speed and agility of smaller teams. And it continues to build the case for scalability.

It's Scalable Because Growth Increases the Validity of Feedback.

A few years ago, a friend from a larger agency was touring The Phelps Group. Standing at the top of the stairs, he looked down from the 2nd floor into our Ballroom (which holds our agency at its present size and whose name is derived its name from being the home of our BrainBangers' Ball and said, "I love your BrainBangers' Ball. It's a powerful tool. But, Joe, what will you do when you have 300 people?"

This challenged me. I didn't have an answer for him.
So I thought about it, off and on, for months.

Then one day, some of us were at The Wall critiquing a team's ad that was aimed at adult women. We looked at the comments on the layout and realized that the opinions of the agency's women were more insightful and therefore more important than our comments. It dawned on me then that as we grow larger, we'll get larger sample sizes from our associates and these larger sample sizes will contain more of the actual intended targets.

We can get comments from the older associates for cruise ship advertising. We can get comments from associates who are parents, or outdoor sports enthusiasts or whatever target's opinion is most pertinent to the project at hand.

There will be more people commenting at The Wall. We can divide The Ball into different groups depending on the work at hand. And our eBangers' – our name for internal email queries on our work – will deliver even more valuable results.

Bring on the growth. The concept just keeps getting stronger!

Possibly the *Most* Scalable Model?

In the *teams-bathed-in-feedback* model, management's role
is to:

- Establish the company's vision and continually
  confirm buy-in
- Ensure that qualified associates are recruited and
  properly deployed
- Ensure that associates are committed to the
  philosophies of continual feedback
- Provide the resources for these people to deliver
  excellent client service

When these conditions exist, there should be no limit as
to how many self-directed teams can exist in an agency.

Growth does not compromise efficiency, individual
freedom, trust, accountability or alignment. Growth
improves the validity of the feedback.

Therefore, *the self-directed teams working in a full-feedback
environment* model is definitely scalable. In fact, for a
professional service organization, it may be the most
scalable model to date.

Conversely, due to changing needs of their employees and the professional service needs of their clients, the model that's been *traditionally* assumed as scalable (command-and-control pyramid structures) is becoming dysfunctional and counterproductive.

The last three sections of this book serve the following purposes:

"The case for IMC" details how to develop and execute media-neutral and discipline-neutral marketing communication plans.

"In the spirit of our mission" and "To achieve our vision" explain the mission and vision of The Phelps Group and how they relate to the holistic design of this overall concept.

Part Three:
The Case for IMC

Self-directed teams

Operating from a full-feedback environment

Delivering IMC

"A brand is a singular idea that exists in the minds and hearts of consumers. A singular idea that happens best when all communications speak with one voice."

Howie Cohen

What is IMC?

Integrated Marketing Communications (IMC) means different things to different people. Here are some examples from the most respected experts on the subject:

"It's a new way of looking at the whole, where before we only saw parts such as advertising, public relations, sales promotion, employee communications, etc."

> *Don E. Schultz, professor of IMC, Northwestern University (one of his definitions)*

"It's the managing of all sources of information about a product which behaviorally moves the customer toward a sale and maintains loyalty."

> *Clark Caywood, former chair of Northwestern University's IMC department*

"Integrated marketing is a cross-functional process for managing profitable brand relationships by bringing people and corporate learning together in order to maintain strategic consistency in brand communications, facilitate purposeful dialogue with customers and other stakeholders, and market a corporate mission that increases brand trust."

> *Tom Duncan, University of Colorado, IMC thought leader and author of the book "Driving Brand Values"*

The Case for IMC

A popular definition is that IMC is the coordination of all the communication tools so that the company speaks with one voice.

At The Phelps Group our definition of IMC is, "IMC is delivering the right message, at the right time and place, to the right market segment, to build the brand, drive sales and provide a feedback loop for improved products and relationships."

We express the heart of this definition with our company mantra:
"All communications. One voice."

We are cognizant of the fact that integrated marketing communications (IMC), is usually a minority part of the entire integrated marketing (IM) mix.

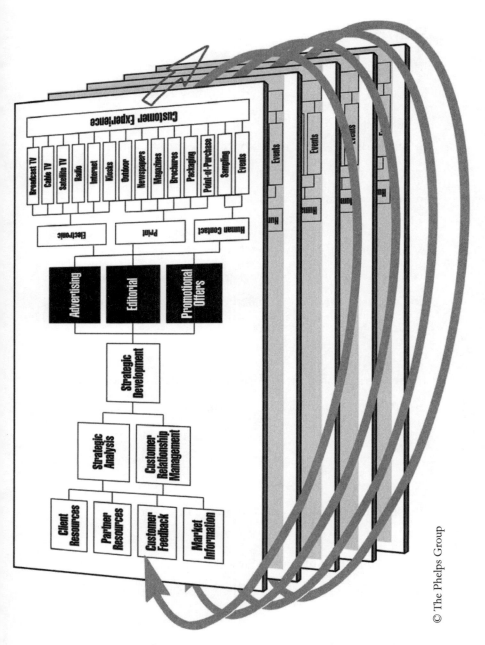

© The Phelps Group

Our challenge at The Phelps Group is to develop IMC programs that provide upward-spiraling, continuously improving platforms to build brands, generate sales and improve the experiences of our clients' customers'.

Why IMC?

More than $200 billion (that's $200,000,000,000!) was spent in 2002 in the U.S. on marketing communications. With people being bombarded by so much commercial information, how can you expect to get your customers' attention unless you're *relentlessly* consistent and efficient in the placement of your message?

Whether it's a TV commercial, an in-store promotion, a website or editorial in a newspaper, most often people don't consciously differentiate between the media they absorb. They just consume the messages.

It's repetition that burns a brand's message into the mind of customers. That's why it's called *branding.*

IMC reflects how the customer sees it — as a flow of information about a company or product from indistinguishable sources. One brand, one voice.

Advertising and publicity. Many consumers, believe it or not, think advertising and publicity are the same thing! Many consumers don't stop to think about whether a company paid a PR specialist to place an article they just read in a magazine. Some people even grant an advertisement the same credibility they give to an editorial written by an independent third party.

All information about a company combines *systematically* in the mind of a consumer as a "brand." The way people formulate ideas about brands is a natural process. What happens when messages are integrated? What happens when they're not? *Consistency and integration promote clarity. Inconsistency promotes confusion.*

Natural *systems* are the most powerful. An animal's body is a system. A cow is a system. You can't cut a cow in half and expect it to produce milk. So it follows that you can't cut a marketing communications program apart and expect it to perform at its highest level.

Using our work for Tahiti Tourisme to illustrate this point: Our position is that the Tahiti experience is *beyond the ordinary*. So, by placing editorial that covers experiences that are beyond the ordinary, by placing ads that promise beyond the ordinary experiences, and by fielding promotions that are not ordinary, we consistently repeat our position to build Tahiti's brand appeal as a vacation spot for people seeking new experiences.

To minimize entropy (the disorder of a system) and maximize syntropy (the alignment of energy and form), marketing communications must be integrated into one seamless system.

Integration increases message consistency. Consistency helps people remember. Together they help the message stand out from the plethora of communications we receive.

A Better Mousetrap Just Isn't Good Enough.

The product or service is the most important element in the marketing mix. However, good products fail daily. I remember the first line in the first chapter of one of my business textbooks in college in the sixties was, "Build a better mousetrap and the world will beat a path to your door." That's laughable nowadays, isn't it?

Why did Sony's Betamax – a superior technology – lose to VHS? Why did Apple's platform – a superior technology – lose out to DOS, and later to Windows?

In both cases, the Matsushita and IBM consortium did a better job of integrating manufacturing and distribution resources in their industry to create more powerful offerings to the consumer.

The same principles apply to marketing communications.

People buy based on what they see, hear—and most importantly, feel – about the brand. Today people have more choices than ever. As products move toward parity in features and price, purchases become emotionally driven. Experts now claim that virtually all purchase and brand

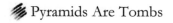

decisions are driven by emotion. People make emotion-based decisions and then build the logic to justify the decision.

To market a product or service properly, marketers need to know how people *feel* about their brands. They are accountable for delivering a return on the company's investment. So, in order to find out how the customers feel and to be able to measure the return on the marketing investment, true IMC creates a response loop.

Response loops are behavior-based and can draw feedback from customers in many ways:

- Customer surveys done in a variety of ways, through various mediums.
- Controlled measurement of actual purchase and use behavior.

These feedback loops help marketers:

- Improve the features and quality of the products they sell.
- Offer the right products or services with the right features to the right people at the right time.
- Understand their customers' needs and desires.
- Gain insight into other products that interest their customers.
- Reap profit more quickly and build more for the long term.

This feedback loop creates real-time, immediate, projectable, *behavior*-based primary research.

This is much more valuable than surveys that simply predict consumer activity by asking about their intentions to buy.

Survey questions are *ninety-pound weaklings* compared to behavior-based information!

Marcom Is Only Part of the Marketing Mix.

Marketing communications is only a piece of the total marketing mix, and just one element of what actually builds the brand in the mind of the consumer. Dr. Tom Duncan explains the situation in his book, *Driving Brand Value.*

Understand the difference between advertising and brand communications:

There are four major types of *Brand Messages:*

1. *Product messages* – all product elements – price points, distribution points, and product performance – have a common dimension.
2. *Support services* – customer services, tech support, after-market follow-up. If customers' communication with a company is negative after a purchase is made, the brand relationship is weakened and the chance of repurchase unlikely.
3. *Unplanned* – what is said in the media and trade journals (not placed by media relations specialists) and what one customer says to another. What special interest groups and government agencies say about a brand can be powerful brand messages, as they are seen as objective third parties.
4. *Marketing communications* – although important in creating awareness and trial, a hundred of these messages can be drowned out by just one product, service or unplanned message. Herein lies the agency's challenge.

Since communications is only one of the four brand
messages, it follows that the agency must be the client's
partner in monitoring all brand messages in order for the
mother-of-all-business models to exist: true Integrated
Marketing (IM).

Mass Marketing Is Past Marketing.

Mass marketing sold standardized mass-produced products to a similarly standardized, undifferentiated mass of consumers. Mass marketing was:

- Top-down – We know what's good for you (and profitable for us!)
- Company-out – We developed it; produced it. It must be good. Buy it.
- Product-oriented – Aren't these terrific features!
- Consumer wishes *not* the highest priority – Remember "New Coke"?

Ad agencies learned about the *product*, then did the advertising – without enough understanding of the customers' point of view.

But, you might ask "What if you're selling toothpaste? Everyone buys it. So mass marketing applies – right?"

Maybe – but, less so every day. Remember when there were a handful of brands, with one product behind each brand?

Crest was Crest. Period. Go to the market now and see Crest for sensitive teeth, Crest to make your teeth whiter,

Crest in a container that stands up by itself. Crest in the squeeze tube. It goes on. And that's just Crest!

The products are differentiated to appeal to different market segments. And to be efficient and effective, each segment is reached via different media.

Consumer is King (and Queen).

The new consumer viewpoint is more like this:

Products increasingly are at parity.
"I have a choice of products that give me the features I want."

The consumer is empowered by information.
"I often know more than the retail salespeople."

People choose what they listen to.
"I want the information when and where I need it."

They talk back and make themselves heard!
"Better listen to me; I've got alternatives."

The market has changed – forever. And for the better.

Let's get to know The Royal Family!

"IBU" and the Rise of Niche Marketing.

Information has empowered the marketers, too. The computer gave companies the power to collect, store, access and manipulate data, to turn that data into information, and then use that information to create the most effective strategies.

So now, agencies first must learn about the customers' *desires* – primarily based on *behavior* and secondarily on other sources like surveys, anecdotal information and customer service reports – and then craft the communication.

Howie Cohen, of The Phelps Group, coined the acronym *IBU* – meaning "I *be* you." Or, "I am you," which expresses the idea that a message has a better likelihood of being noticed if it communicates the thought "I understand your needs because I *understand you*." This is an update on the industry's former creed, coined by Rosser Reeves in the 1950s, that the first step in determining the message is to find the product's USP (Unique Selling Proposition). The USP is still important as a point of differentiation. It simply must be in answer to a customer-driven desire.

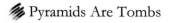

We must know what the consumer really wants – then be the one they think of for that feature.

Comprehensive, reliable information about the customer is now readily available and accessible as never before. We can look much closer at customer behavior. Demographic, psychographic, and lifestyle information is abundant. Focus groups and other qualitative research devices get more sophisticated every year. We can measure "emotional affinity." This enables niche marketing to replace mass marketing.

The downside of all this is *information overload*. The objective is to turn the information into knowledge that is actionable. Zeroing in on which data to analyze is increasingly important.

Finding out what the consumer wants and claiming the clients' products have it, raises the subject of Truth. At The Phelps Group, our *highest value* and our *mission* keep us on course.

We commit to *Truth as our highest value*. Our work influences millions of people daily. Therefore, truth must be our guiding light.

Our mission is to do great work for *deserving* clients. We define a deserving client as one whose products enrich the lives of those who buy them.

So, our job is somewhat simplified. We simply need to find the *truth*. And then clearly articulate that truth in a memorable way.

It's a good thing we have great clients, because that challenge alone is plenty taxing!

The Four Ps Have Given Way to the Four Cs.

Business is really just about buying and selling things. Marketing is about finding out what people want and giving it to them.

The four Ps of marketing – Product, Price, Place and Promotion – were written from the producers' point of view. The mindset for marketers now has to be the mindset of the *consumer*. A few years ago the professors of IMC at Northwestern University said it best when they replaced the four Ps with the four Cs.

Product	*is now*	Consumer wants and needs
Price	*is now*	Cost to satisfy the consumer's need
Place	*is now*	Convenience to buy
Promotion	*is now*	Communication

Product: Contemporary thinking is that a company's greatest asset is most often its customer base. That being the case, fulfilling the *Consumer's* desires is more important than continuing to sell your current products. A case in point is Blockbuster's transition from renting videotapes to selling other movie delivery systems like DirecTV.

Price: With time being our most precious commodity, the time it takes to purchase becomes an important part of the *Cost*. "Paying a 50% higher price point at my corner convenience store may, in fact, be less expensive than spending the time required to go to a large supermarket."

Place: "My telephone or Internet connection may be much more *Convenient* for me than your traditional retail outlet."

Promotion: "Don't 'sell' me. Just deliver a quick, clear Communication of the pertinent information, make me an offer – and I'll make the decision." The word promotion worked because it started with a "P". The problem is that in marketing terminology, a promotion is an offer. And promotions are just one leg of the 3-legged marcom stool, which is supported by advertising (paid), editorial (non-paid) and promotions (an offer). So let's call it what it is: Marketing *Communications*. Then to be effective, the communication must be relevant to the consumer and hold the target's attention.

Why Don't More Companies Practice IMC?

Integrating all marketing communication messages is just common sense. So why don't more agencies and companies practice IMC? If this is what everyone wants, why aren't there more campaigns that are consistent throughout all points of customer contact? Why aren't there more closed feedback loops for continuous improvement?

Here's the answer for most cases:

In larger companies, communications disciplines are often departmentalized – a public relations department, an advertising department, a promotions department, a direct marketing department or an interactive department. Quite often, these marketing-related departments report to different people. (Example: a company where the Web site is controlled by MIS, or where the advertising people report to marketing and public relations reports directly to the president.)

To make it worse, different *outside agencies* and companies are hired to assist with, or drive, each of these disciplines. Personnel in each of these areas are typically compensated in direct proportion to the amount of money that flows through their area. This sets up a natural phenomenon known as "turf wars" or "silos" – the outcome of which are not necessarily aligned with what's best for the long-term benefit of the client of the company.

To counter this, companies can take active steps to ensure that their marketing communications funds are spent in their best interests by organizing marketing communications personnel around the internal "client" to eliminate – or at the very least, drastically reduce – conflict.

On the company side, the internal "clients" are the corporate brand and the product line brands. Marketing communications specialists who are organized in teams can best support these areas, as opposed to those organized in single-discipline departments. The objectives of the marcom teams will then be aligned with their internal clients' goals.

On the agency side, you won't find the proper organization to achieve IMC in a traditional ad agency. They are organized to sell and produce advertising. Advertising may not be what's best for the job at hand. Maybe the solution is editorial coverage or promotional offers. Most often, it's a carefully balanced and coordinated mix.

Nor will you find a conflict-free situation in a public relations agency, a sales promotion company, a direct-mail house or a new media firm. They all *sell what they have* – not necessarily what their clients most need.

Truly integrated marketing communications will, most likely, be found only in a company or agency organized for true integration. An organization that fosters alignment of purpose. One that has committed to executing constantly improving, consistent campaigns. One, which is *organized to recommend what's best for the client.*

Organized to Recommend What's Best For the Client.

An IMC company, organized *around the client*, without profit-center-related conflict of interest, has a greater propensity to offer more *media-neutral* insights, strategies and programs. Traditionally organized PR agencies and ad agencies are less likely to make recommendations outside their scope of services.

An IMC company can be its client's objective consultant *and* be best qualified to execute the recommended program. Unlike a traditional consultancy, it actually has the marcom resources needed to develop creative materials, produce and distribute the message and measure the effectiveness.

Whole-Life-Branding™.

The Phelps Group believes in something Howie Cohen, our creative coach, labeled "Whole-Life-Branding." It recognizes that there's a new consumer out there. One whose fundamental beliefs have been shaken.

It seemed to hit all at once starting in 2001. From terrorist attacks to 401K meltdowns to greedy accounting tactics and the sins of the Catholic Church, consumers have felt betrayed (disappointed, confused and angered) and they're looking for something new in the brands that they choose – something to believe in. Brands that aren't just trying to sell them something. But are interested in becoming an integral part of their lives – their whole lives.

Here are the four requirements of a Whole Life Brand:

- Life Affirming – they enrich the lives of those who buy them.
- Simplicity – appreciation of simple pleasures.
- Honesty – they represent themselves truthfully.
- Connectivity – supporting your values and beliefs (family, church, community, etc.)

Connectivity connects all the dots – consumer, product, neighborhood, beliefs and values. An example is Target stores.

191

Target donates 10% of their profits to charity. That's going beyond selling me products. It's connecting my purchase, to my values, to my causes and my beliefs. Our client, PETCO, connects my love for animals with a drive to save animals' lives and find homes for them.

In a world where new competitors are springing up everywhere and brand loyalty is waning, Whole-Life-Branding has the potential to create brand loyalty, repeat business and the rare privilege of having a "customer for life."

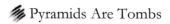

CRM Is Forcing Our Morphing to a Direct Response Mentality.

As we review the IMC programs we're developing for our clients, we see that virtually everything we do now in advertising and promotions has a response device attached to it. Why? For one thing, it's *because we can.* And because conversations with our customers are valuable, we will. These ongoing conversations are the lifeblood of Customer Relationship Management (CRM). CRM is a mindset. It's not something you can departmentalize. It must be infused throughout the entire organization.

Tom Duncan warns, "CRM is too often used to find new ways to bombard and push good customers to the point where they want to tell the company to shove it."

As a consumer, I agree with him.

Cynthia Clotzman, our CRM coach, wrote:
> "At its core, CRM is about maximizing the value that a business gives the customer while maximizing the value that the customer gives the business."

CRM focuses on customers across all areas of the company, integrating sales, marketing, and customer service functions – basically any function that "touches" the customer.

Computerization, aided by the Web, is making it more feasible to track customer behavior and company performance to allow more accurate analysis.

Because of demand for accountability, and because direct response has permeated virtually every marcom discipline, we want a direct response mentality to permeate every individual and account team in our agency. Less so for media relations, because there is no guarantee that an editor or producer will run a phone number or Web address. But editorial placements often do generate immediate sales results. Rosie O'Donnell featured the Tickle Me Elmo doll on her show and the response to the manufacturer was immediate. Another example, is when our agency's PR work for Teva Sandals increased Web sales exponentially via traffic generated from editorial placements.

This focus on CRM has had numerous effects on our company, our mindset and the experience and skills required to deliver the service our clients deserve.

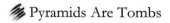

Regarding our <u>mindset</u>: This relates directly to the first tenet of our mission which is, "To do great work…." We define *great work* as that which builds the brand while creating sales impact. The mindset that traditional advertising is basically for brand-building is obsolete.

Traditional advertising increasingly will be expected to illicit response. So as we've pursued our holy grail of great work, we've discovered and proven that the typical "junk mail" look of direct marketing is not necessary or even desirable to create response. We've proven that we can create image-building campaigns that have strong direct response elements.

An example of this occurred when Renaissance Cruises came to us for help with their direct response campaign.

Their direct mail piece was designed in the spirit of the often-used direct mail adage "ugly sells." Which in some cases, it does. Renaissance, however, was selling a quality product to high-income, highly educated people. In our first test, we used the elements from their control (best performing) piece, and designed them into a much cleaner self-mailer. When we tested the new design against the old design in a split run, the new design beat the cluttered one by an increase in responses of over 30%. This was reassuring for us, because it was more valid proof that direct mail doesn't have to look schlocky to be effective.

Regarding the talent required to create this double-duty work: (build brands while generating sales.) It is essential that every member on our teams understands the need to produce measurable, results-generating work. Our copywriters and art directors know, respect and use the basic principles required to generate response. Because of the information that now is flowing back to us from our clients' customers as a result of our work, each team has developed, to differing degrees, the ability to analyze the data and apply it to the next round of work.

It's this analysis of *behavior* that can deliver insight for better customer understanding. It measures and predicts actual consumer *behavior*, as opposed to the less accurate method of measuring consumer attitudes from which behavioral activities are predicted. For example the correlation between "intent to purchase" and actual purchases is not nearly as accurate as predicting future purchases based on actual purchases.

The premise here is that for maximum power, direct response no longer can afford to be a discrete discipline within an agency. It's become apparent that every marketing communications specialist must, to a degree, become a direct response specialist in their area of expertise to excel.

- Art directors must know how to build brand with images while guiding the eye to the response mechanism.
- Writers must know how to build the desire plus trigger the action.
- Media specialists must buy for *response* as well as reach and frequency.
- A promotional offer is, of course, measured by its response level as well as its brand-building power.
- Journalists want to give their readers, viewers and listeners more information. So media relations specialists need to inform them about free brochure offers or websites with more information.

Direct mail, direct response TV and e-commerce are not necessarily discrete disciplines. They're simply related to the specific delivery systems of the mail, broadcast, cable and the Web.

Client-based, self-directed teams are in alignment with this mindset. Stop and think for a moment how hard this level of integrated CRM would be to achieve within a company organized in functional departments.

It's probably obvious by now – you can't separate CRM from IMC. It all needs to work together in one seamless system. As the data from our clients' customers flows back to us at an ever increasing rate and volume, we must be able to organize, analyze and extract fresh insights to discover new market segments and measure demand for new products and product modifications. To this end, we are experiencing increased demand for people who can analyze this data and deliver insights into customer behavior. After all, successful creative strategies are usually triggered by new customer insights.

Is this analysis the front end or the back end of the process? It's both, because as you can see by our chart at the beginning of this section, the continuous improvement process is circular in nature. The results (back end) feed directly into the development of the next program (front end). This is where the past meets the future. Er, uh, I guess that would be *now*?

This is marketing's *flash point*. Proper focus on this area can turn incremental improvement into *perpetual evolution* .

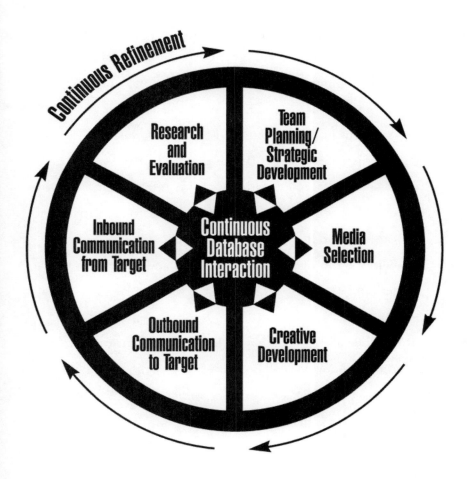

Database management is at the heart of customer relationship management (CRM). And it's an integral part of every step in the marketing communications process.

CRM: The Superior Experience.

One of our goals is to help our clients create a superior experience for their customers and thereby improve their customer relationships. This goes beyond traditional marketing communications. It reaches deep into our clients' operational issues. Dr. Tom Duncan's main message to us in a presentation to our agency was that *customer service is where business is going*. So, to be true consultants and partners with our clients, we must be committed to helping them improve their customer service. We'll accomplish this by bringing the full complement of capabilities – through our own resources and those of our partners and suppliers.

CRM will be a key to success in the upcoming customized economy. Companies will benefit when true integration of the marcom disciplines encourages *systemic* application of CRM throughout all communications.

Dell Computers believes the customer experience, and therefore CRM, is the key to its current and future success. They formed the Customer Experience Council to scrutinize how Dell interacts with its customers. Dell gets millions of customer contacts a week in the form of emails, deliveries, phone calls, returns and so forth. The council's job is to figure out how to monitor and measure the quality of those contacts and to instill commitment to a superior customer experience in Dell's employees.

Jack Daly, the renowned motivational speaker, told us about a car salesman who took Jack's picture in front of his new Mazda Miata when he sold it to him. Shortly thereafter, Jack received a thank you note with the picture enclosed. Later, he received a calendar with the photo on it. The salesman's "touch" campaign went on and on. And as Jack said, "Who do you think I thought of when it was time for me to buy a new car?!"

Customer relationship management: CRM. In concept, it's not new. Successful companies have been doing it since the beginning of commerce. The difference now is that more and more products are at parity. It's service that makes the difference. There are software programs to help us do it better. So, to be successful, we must be organized and committed to providing that service.

A Word About Words:

Terms related to direct and CRM are often mistakenly interchanged. Here's a short primer on the subject:

- *Direct response:* paid marcom messages that contain response mechanisms.
- *Direct mail:* Marcom messages sent via mail to customers.
- *DRTV:* Direct response messages sent via broadcast, satellite or cable TV.
- *Database management:* Building and managing a body of information about individuals and groups.
- *Direct marketing:* Eliciting sales directly from the end consumer.
- *E-commerce:* Online sales.

IMC At Work.

We've been practicing IMC at The Phelps Group for over two decades now. Elements of the proof of its success are that we are the agency-of-record for more than a dozen clients who are the leader in their respective industries.

When we don't handle the entire marketing communications package for a client, we ask our clients to encourage intra-agency communications to facilitate proper integration of disciplines.

Our client retention record is far above industry norms, and for good reason: *Our work gets results.*

How IMC Works – Day to Day.

The IMC team sets a marketing communications objective (what we want to *achieve*). From that, an overall communications strategy is developed (*what* we'll *say* to achieve it). From that, a creative strategy will emerge (*how* we'll say it). These strategies may utilize PR, advertising, sales promotions – or any combination of these disciplines.

Is the job of each discipline tougher and more restrictive when it's agreed that they must be consistent with the other? You bet it is! If advertising or PR can do its own thing without considering the ramifications for the other disciplines, then their job is easier – and probably quicker.

There are instances – most often related to a less-than-adequate budget – where one discipline, say for example public relations, is all that can be deployed effectively.

However, in most instances it's best to launch a campaign that uses a variety of tools to reach the prospect at different contact points and have them all work together to communicate consistent core product benefits and brand image.

The coordination and alignment of these elements is often considered the greatest challenge for marketing communications companies, but it also offers the greatest opportunities for success.

Integration Saves Money.

A few years back, at one of our agency's Spring Advances we were challenged by some Outward Bound exercises.

The problem-solving exercises had time limits. So the teams jumped in quickly and just started *doing*, before we were in agreement with *what* we were doing. Finally, after two days of those exercises – and loads of frustration – it started to sink in that the investment of time early on to plan and integrate the strategy and tactics was well worth it.

This is somewhat related to the carpenter's adage to "measure twice, cut once."

Here's a situation: Imagine that a group of marcom specialists representing the advertising, PR, promotions, direct, media and interactive disciplines and billing at an average rate of $XXX per hour, have reviewed a client's situation. They've agreed on the communications strategy that the consumers who now believe "Y" must be influenced to believe "Z." And now it's time to determine how to change perceptions.

One of the specialists, let's say an advertising copywriter, has an idea. It's clever, but not quite on strategy, so it limits the opportunities for PR and promotions. Discussion ensues. Then a PR person comes up with a novel approach. The group likes it, and decides to allow the advertising and promotions specialists time to develop an approach consistent with the media relations portion of the campaign. So the group schedules to reconvene a few days later to move the project to the next step.

Is this a complicated and laborious situation? Yes. Is it one that is necessary to align the disciplines and achieve continual forward motion? We believe so.

Expensive? Yes, in the short term. Is it worth it? Yes. Because it *saves* the client money in the long term.

How expensive would it have been for the advertising specialists to proceed with development of their concept, and find out later that it didn't lend itself to a consistent campaign because it didn't work for the other disciplines? How expensive would it be if an incredible opportunity that maximized the power of the other disciplines had been lost?

Timing is another reason for integration. For example, journalists want *news*. Too often the news is announced in an ad. That makes it harder to position the information as news with journalists doesn't it?

Employee relations are another reason. How many times have companies launched a new campaign without informing the sales force or the front-line customer service personnel?

We believe the more you invest in up-front planning for integration, the better the ROI in the longer term. Who can argue with that?

However, it's amazing how often companies don't follow IMC planning processes. Some ad agencies have never even met the people at the PR agency working on the same account!

One of the greatest challenges in developing IMC is adhering to processes that increase the odds of producing the best multi-pronged programs – programs centered around a core benefit, with original and motivating messages that generate healthy participation by the target audience.

Pay Now – Or Pay More Later.

Who pays for the additional time required for proper integration?

Over the years, as we've developed our client-based IMC model at The Phelps Group, we have spent countless unbillable hours in meetings trying to align the disciplines to speak with one voice for a client. These hours can be categorized into three areas:

1. Time invested in devising our method of operations.
2. The hours spent inventing the processes to make IMC programs happen – where we've worked out the real world kinks not covered in a textbook.
3. Time invested in cross-training.

It's remarkable how differently people of diverse marcom disciplines think, most notably advertising people as compared with PR people. Cross-training helps bridge the gap in understanding, and eventually anticipating what needs to happen for proper integration.

Time Wasted.

Over the years, integration has forced us to learn the
importance of time management for meetings. So we know
that for most companies, as integration becomes more of
an issue, so will time management. Our time, as related to
integration might be categorized as:

1. Time lost – which could have been avoided with
   proper meeting management.
2. Time invested – developing true integration by
   improving our processes.
3. Time spent together working on the integration of
   our clients' marcom.

Who pays for the additional time required for item 3
above?

The client might think, "If I buy all these services from one
agency, I'd expect them to come up with something that all
works together, and not charge extra for it." The agency
side might say, "To be competitive with single-discipline
competitors, we have to keep our margins thin. But
delivery of quality IMC requires additional time. It's not as
easy as developing just an advertising campaign or an
editorial angle to pitch."

The answer as to what is fair lies in the particulars of a client/agency relationship. So, if both sides are aware of the processes and appreciate the additional time required to develop proper IMC programs, there's a better chance of striking a fair arrangement. And the ROI can be healthy for both sides.

Another good exercise to contrast the inefficiencies of having separate agencies for each of the disciplines with IMC:

In the multiple agency scenario, each agency has account management which should be leading its team through the situation analysis, establishing objectives, determining targets and messages, measuring results and making unbiased recommendations. If a client has a different agency for the disciplines of advertising, direct, public relations, promotions and interactive, not only are there significant redundancies in the tasks listed above, but there can be a problem with inconsistent targets, messages and timing because the right hand isn't coordinated with the left. Financial and creative turfs get protected. It's what is called the "not invented here" syndrome. (If it's the other agency's idea, it can't be as good as ours.) The result is that developing and implementing consistent programs becomes like herding cats!

Conversely, on a self-directed IMC team, you have one team leader and the member's goals are in alignment. Whatever it takes for the client's success also will be good for the team.

That's *efficiency*. And in the end, the client gets the best value from this organizational model.

"Pick Two" Went Out With the Three Stooges.

As noted earlier in Part One, the adage "Faster, better, cheaper: Pick two." no longer applies. Now it's faster, better, cheaper *and* integrated! Pick all four, or your competition will deliver it ahead of you – and hand you your head while they're at it.

So what's it worth to have all points of contact with the consumer working in unison toward the same positioning to deliver measurable results?

It's the marketing director's dream to have a seamless program. It's the stockholder's dream, because often their sole interest is ROI. So the early investment of additional time required to align the marcom disciplines will never be questioned once the power of their integration is allowed to come to fruition.

It's All About the Work.

There's no substitute for great work: fresh customer insights, brilliant creativity and beautiful design, executed flawlessly that achieves positive results.

As we all learn to work in teams, to contribute to projects in a collaborative fashion and to have other people's welfare dependent upon our personal performance, we can take guidance from Dan Wieden, of the Wieden and Kennedy ad agency. I understand that he once had a sign over his desk that said, "Be regular and orderly in your life, so that you may be violent and original in your work."

I take that to mean: Get the research to back it up – then be *bold!*

At The Phelps Group, we *define* great work as marketing communications that builds the brand while creating immediate sales impact. Another way we say it is that "Great work is a refreshing jolt to the psyche that gets results."

We can make lists of elements that are typically present in great work: strong emotional appeal; appeal to the rational;

a unique look and feel; enhanced customer relationships; and the message being from the consumer point of view. We could go on. Books have been written on what makes for great communications.

Ultimately, it's not about how funny it is, or how original it is – or how many awards it has won.

Whether it's media relations, advertising or promotions, great work in marketing communications is best defined by its *results* – both long- and short-term.

The way to measure the value of marketing communications most often has been to measure its appeal to a panel of experts in an industry awards contest, or a change in attitude on the part of the consumer. Asking about "intent to buy" or, "did the advertising influence your decision?" is most often not a valid measurement of a program's value.

A better way to measure value is to measure an actual change in *behavior* by the consumer.

The quest in our industry is to maximize our potentials by removing obstacles that get in the way of the best work –

and by finding new methods to improve the creative development process.

So much time in our industry is spent conjecturing, pontificating, pondering and, in the end, *guessing* what the impact of an effort (message, offer and medium) will be. We increasingly recommend that *tests* are worth the time and money. They minimize risks by reducing the initial investment. The Internet is making this more feasible – time-wise and money-wise.

So, if you believe it will work – stop talking about it and test it!

On Producing Better Work.

As we all learn to work in teams, to contribute to projects in a collaborative fashion and to have other people's welfare dependent upon our personal performance, it helps to remember that because we're accountable for our work we typically strive to deliver more than we promise.

It's our intention to deliver more than we promise – to under promise and over deliver – because we've found that happiness results when reality exceeds someone's level of expectation.

The success of our agency is dependent upon our ability to estimate properly, get agreement on the estimate and produce the goods as promised. In order for a job to be estimated properly, it must be properly planned. If it's planned properly, the estimate can be accurate. Then, this estimate must be properly explained to our client. If the proper estimate is approved, it's usually a joy to produce from that point. The budget enables us to use the right tools and spend the time necessary to produce a quality product.

It's often expensive in the *short* run to do a job right. But, the rewards for great work are long term. Remember the adage: "The sweet taste of high quality lingers long after the bitterness of the high price has faded." In fact, when marketing communications are done correctly, they are not an expense – they are an investment in the company's brand.

Because it's so easy to underestimate how much time it takes to produce great work, and because inflation erodes the value of the dollar, it's normal for us all to experience sticker shock at the cost of the work we do.

This can result in the fear of presenting an estimate that reflects the real costs of doing quality work. This fear causes the downfall of many projects – and companies. The fear of a competitor being able to do the job for less is one thing that tends to undermine confidence. But we must remember that, generally, we are not on a per-project basis with our clients.

We are the agency-of-record, which should reflect a higher level of trust. Therefore, if we show our clients that we have taken the time to plan the job properly, searched for the suppliers offering the best value, and that the project will give them a good return on their investment, they have no incentive to listen to or solicit bids from other suppliers (who may low-ball the price just to get their first order).

And, just as we ask for the right to make a reasonable profit, we respect that same right for our suppliers. In general, we are not interested in one-shot deals with suppliers. We want to build long-term, mutually profitable relationships with our suppliers.

How to Achieve "Group Genius."

As it relates specifically to advertising, the history of creative development as it pertains to organizational structure is an interesting one. From the beginning of modern advertising up until the Sixties, the copy/contact person from the agency visited the client, determined what the message would be, then turned that over to the agency's graphics department for visuals and typesetting. Relative to today's norms, little creative collaboration took place, and the results are obvious when you look at advertising from that period. However, media was not as fragmented as it is today, and competition for the consumer's eyes and ears was tame compared to today's.

In the 1960s, Bill Bernbach and a few others on Madison Avenue pioneered the creative team approach that exists in most agencies today that produce quality work. It works like this: The account executive or the account planner, delivers an advertising strategy (i.e., what is to be communicated) to a copywriter/art director team. This two-person team then bounces ideas back and forth to produce visuals and headlines that work together as a single concept. The synergy of the two minds intensely working together produces a 1+1=3 phenomenon. This approach elevated the quality of work in the industry to a new high. This more sophisticated approach was necessitated by the fact that the ever-increasing level of advertising "noise" made it tougher for advertisers to have their message heard over the clutter of other advertisers.

However, in today's fragmented media market, advertising alone isn't as effective as it was in the past.

Enter client-team-based IMC: When strategy, art, copy, PR, promotion, interactive and media specialists collaborate to develop integrated campaigns, challenges are seen from numerous points of view. Ideas spark other ideas. Then, results-oriented campaigns are born that work with a variety of media. It's all communications speaking with one voice.

The phenomenon is more like $1+1+1+1+1+1=15$. Group genius at work.

Eliminate Organization-induced Conflicts.

If a client goes to an advertising agency with a marketing communications challenge, the agency will almost always recommend *advertising*. If the same client goes to a PR agency with a challenge, they'll almost always suggest what they have to sell – PR. The same is true for direct marketing and promotions companies. Most companies will sell you what they have – not necessarily what is best for the situation. Because as the saying goes, *"If all you have is a hammer, every problem looks like a nail."*

The same conflict exists when an agency is organized in functional departments. A director heads the department, and the director's compensation is determined by the amount of billing flowing through the department. The natural tendency is for the director or their people to want to maximize the department's percentage of the client's budget. They too often resent being included in meetings they can't bill time for – thus reducing collaboration and integration. So whose best interests are being served? The client's? Often not.

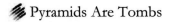

These conflicts of interest waste energy and produce anxiety. Both are detrimental to productivity and a healthy business environment.

Deployment in client-centered teams eliminates conflict of interest and aligns the members in purpose to achieve the client's goals.

People should never be confused about whether they're working for the client or an agency department head. Client-related decisions shouldn't be made because someone wants to make more money for his or her department.

Conversely, specialists working on client-based teams do what is best for the client. When they help create client success, they will be rewarded for it – at least in the long run.

An Agency Is Only as Good as Its People.

What happens when a client thinks they can't get the individual firepower with an IMC team as with separate agencies? It all depends on the talent levels and the teamwork skills of the individuals on the team that's fielded by the agency.

At a seminar for advertising agency CEOs I attended a few years ago, the moderator asked, "How many of you offer integrated marketing communications services?" Most in the audience raised their hand. I was sitting in the front row, so I jumped up, turned around and asked, "And how many of you offer public relations?" Only two raised their hands out of more than 30 agencies. I then asked, "How can you claim to offer integrated communications if you don't integrate the two most powerful marcom disciplines – advertising and public relations?" A fellow from one of the Madison Avenue agencies offered, "We can't get good PR people to come to work for an ad agency. They want to work in a PR agency." (Because they don't want to take a back seat to advertising.)

I knew then that those agencies could not achieve true integrated marketing, because they were carrying too much departmental baggage – and could possibly become extinct before they could ever evolve into a successful IMC company.

PR people in a client-based organization learn about and contribute to IMC. As do promotions, interactive, direct, media and other advertising specialists. They like being part of whatever solution is best for the client. They like seeing the bigger picture. And they like the variety that IMC brings to their work life.

When disciplines are organized in departments or divisions – or worse yet, when companies try to fill a void by way of alliances with other companies – you have *segregated, or dis-*integrated marketing. In these instances, financial turf wars are natural to the system – and in conflict with the client's best interests – and, too often, people feel like they're the last to know what's going on.

For true integrated marketing, the organization doing the work – whether it be the client or its agency – will perform better when organized in a way that eliminates fiefdoms and conflicts of interest.

This true alignment of disciplines encourages people to work together for the benefit of their clients.

How to Integrate When Multiple Agencies and Internal Departments Are Involved.

In most situations, all marcom disciplines are not deployed on one customer-focused team. In those instances, someone and/or some function needs to bring the disciplines together at critical times for strategic development and executional alignment.

Common situations are:

- Client marketing department working with one agency.
- Client marketing department working with multiple agencies.
- Multiple internal client departments working with one agency.
- Multiple internal client departments working with multiple agencies.

As you move down the above list, the situations get more complicated and the chances for turf wars and communication breakdown increase.

Often, when multiple organizations work together, they don't draw on each other's strengths and relative points of view to execute a project. The first mistake they usually make is to develop their own situation analysis and move into strategy without thoroughly consulting each other.

Resources are wasted on redundant research and conclusions often based on incomplete information.

Here's a checklist for integrating multiple disciplines:

- Together, build a list of information needed for a thorough situation analysis.
- Together, determine how, when, by whom and on whose budget this information will be mined.
- Together, share the entire body of primary and secondary research.
- Together, develop a strengths, weaknesses, opportunities and threats analysis (SWOT).
- Together, develop a list of conclusions.
- Together, establish objectives.
- Together, brainstorm strategic scenarios using various combinations of disciplines.
- Individually, develop ideas within the disciplines in alignment with the agreed upon strategy.
- Together, determine how these scenarios will be judged for feasibility or tested for ROI.
- Together, develop timetable or critical path.
- Individually, execute the work within the disciplines.
- Together, keep each other current on progress and opportunities to coordinate.
- Together, track, measure and analyze the results.
- Together, determine the next steps to start the second loop of the process.

If you can pull this off, you have found the holy grail of integration. You are in marketing utopia.

The Case for IMC

Note: The next chapter is an outline of the processes we follow when developing IMC programs. Its content is somewhat academic in nature and is meant to be used as a reference and checklist.

IMC Planning
Processes 501

IMC Planning Processes 501.

Most people who have studied marketing and have worked in agencies for years still don't thoroughly understand or don't follow the proven processes in their discipline. That, combined with the fact that we've had to upgrade the processes in order for them to work in an IMC environment, leads us to call it IMC 501 – instead of 101.

Please don't judge that statement as being cavalier, because we admit that we're all too often remiss in the thorough application of our own processes.

We've talked about what IMC is and why it's the most effective way to plan marketing communications. Now, here's the *step-by-step process for developing an IMC plan.*

But before reviewing the planning steps, let it be understood that: Every agency and every marketing textbook has variations in the steps for plan development. The difference is that our processes look at the marcom challenge from a holistic point of view.

We suggest that you know and follow the general processes and teach them to your clients and teammates. And if you can help us improve them, please e-mail your suggestions directly to pyramids@thephelpsgroup.com.

Note: We often hear people using the words objectives, goals, strategies and tactics in different ways. Yet, it's important that we have a common understanding of the differences. So, while it may be elementary for some, we need to confirm that we're all on the same page before we dive into the steps.

Definitions:
1. *Goals* are what we want to accomplish.
2. *Objectives* are goals defined by measurable results.
3. *Strategies* are plans or methods for achieving our objectives. Strategies are *how* we'll do it.
4. *Tactics* are generally the smaller-scale actions that are part of a larger strategy.

The reason it can be so confusing at times is that tactics can become strategies. For example, in the overall context of a war, a bomb is a tactic. But what if it's an atomic bomb? (That qualifies it to be a strategy, right?)

Here are the processes as we have learned, adapted and evolved them to work for IMC:

Situation Analysis.

When traveling, a roadmap is used to determine where we are now. In marketing, this is called the Situation Analysis.

What's the current state of affairs and what recent and future changes do we see in the marketing environment in each of these areas?

- Technology.
- Social/cultural.
- Legal/political.
- Market size: historical, current and projected
- Market share and trends.
- Competitive activities and positioning (real and intended).
- Product features and benefits.
- Pricing and overall cost to consumer.
- Communications to the trade and consumers.
- Distribution and convenience to the consumer.
- Consumer purchase motivations.

Answers to the questions above come from:

- Existing (secondary) internal research.
- New internal data gathering (sales force, store checks).
- Existing research from trade publications, associations and research firms.
- New (primary) research.

Research methods are changing rapidly. Computerization is making it more economically feasible to track consumer behavior. Therefore, it's becoming common to base marketing decisions more on actual behavior and less on consumer attitudes and intentions. Because of this and the proliferation of media choices, the question becomes more "What cells do we put in our test matrix?" and less "What will this year's campaign be?"

Planning based on actual behavior is more stable than projections from attitudes or "intention to buy" numbers.

Questions that must be answered are:

- Will the *consumer* want this?
- At a reasonable *cost* to them?
- Is it *convenient* for them to buy?
- Are we clearly *communicating* our story? (via all the points of contact: packaging, POP, advertising, sales promotions, editorial?)
- Where will society and our industry be in five years?
- How should that affect what we're doing today?

A review of the situation will:

- Confirm successes and failures of the past.
- Spawn insights and conclusions about the future.
- Help you understand "where you are now."

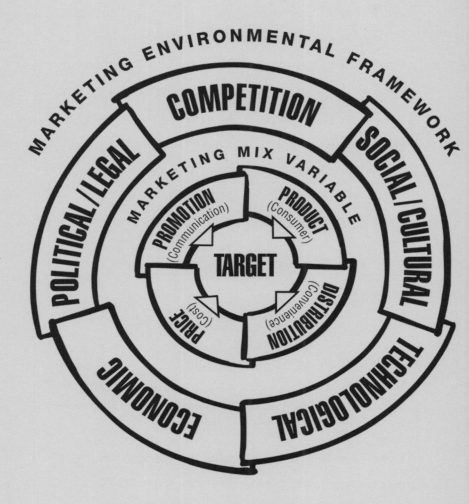

A situation analysis at The Phelps Group considers how the customer relates to the four marketing mix variables in light of the five marketing environment variables. This chart can serve as a quick checklist for the main areas of consideration in a situation analysis for any business. You may download a color version from the Creative Strategies pages at www.thephelpsgroup.com.

© The Phelps Group

How to Develop the Situation Analysis:
Team Planning.

We recognize that the sharpest communications strategies and the best brand-building executions come from having in-depth and up-to-the-minute insights into consumers' heads, hearts and everyday lives. Precisely where and how does a client's brand fit into people's lives? Why should they care about it at all? Why should they choose it in preference to the many other alternatives that are so readily available?

A research specialist who describes the lifestyle and desires of the ultimate consumer to the marcom team is often called an account planner.

We believe in the basic benefits of account planning, where firsthand and detailed knowledge of the consumer's life is brought into the strategic and creative processes. The planner not only understands but also *represents* the consumer to the client-based team and to the client's organization.

The Case for IMC

Account planning works. It succeeds because it digs deep. But we go *beyond* account planning to dig even deeper, better and faster on a client's behalf.

We call it *Team Planning*.

Since we operate in self-directed, client-based teams comprised of IMC specialists, team planning immerses the entire team – not just the research specialist – in the consumer's reality.

Instead of the account planner venturing out alone into the consumer's world and then reporting back to the rest of the agency, team planning uses a planner's expertise to lead the team in experiencing in-depth, face-to-face and ongoing interaction with its client's customers via store checks, focus groups or 1-to-1 interviews.

We encourage all team members to:

- Go through the buying process for our client.
- Go through the buying process for a competitor.
- Use the product.
- Use the competitors' products.
- Call our client's and the competitors' customer service lines.
- Ask a question online.

- Monitor industry user groups and chat rooms.
- Talk to retailers.
- Watch and interview consumers at retail.
- Interview a trade magazine journalist or publisher.
- Interview a consumer magazine journalist.
- Ride with a company sales representative.
- Observe consumer focus groups.
- Speak directly to the participants in the focus groups.

This immersion in the customer and industry world should be an on-going modus operandi throughout the year, with special emphasis just prior to annual planning sessions. It yields true empathy and crucial insights for more relevant and meaningful strategies and creative thinking.

Unlike conventional account planning, which is usually limited to advertising, the team planning approach is applied to every aspect of the marketing communications mix.

The commitment to IMC and the team planning philosophy helps build brands that touch customers at virtually every point of media contact. It helps detect changes in attitudes, demographics and trends. It uncovers organizational and operational problems. This is one more way to put more brains on building the brand.

Conclusions to the Situation Analysis.

We state our conclusions in the form of a prioritized SWOT analysis:

- Strengths
- Weaknesses
- Opportunities
- Threats

This leads to the establishment of marketing objectives for the future.

Marketing Objectives.

Clear and concise measurable objectives are the foundation of the plan. The marketing objectives define *what* we want to do. For example:

> **Situation** – Our distribution is lacking.

> **Objective** – Increase direct sales by 20%.

Or:

> **Situation** – We're high priced with a low quality image.

> **Objective** – Increase customers' perception of our brand quality to equal that of the industry leader.

From these marketing objectives will come:

Marketing Strategies.

Getting more specific about how these objectives will be reached, and staying with the same examples:

Objective: Increase direct sales by 20%.

Strategy: Add direct-to-consumer marketing to the distribution channels via the Web.

Or:

Objective – Increase customers' perception of our brand quality to equal that of the industry leader.

Strategy: Charge higher prices and invest the additional margin in brand-building marcom programs.

Marketing Communications Objectives.

The thinking to establish marcom objectives will follow this line:

- What do our targets believe now?
- What do we want them to think or do?
- What is the message that will change their attitude or spur action?

When we're reasonably sure that we know the answer to the third bullet, we know what we need to communicate. Our communications objective then becomes to deliver that message. For example, here's the logic path we used for our Tahiti Tourisme client:

What they believed: Research showed us that many in our target groups thought Tahiti to be a longer flight than it actually is from Los Angeles.

What we wanted them to believe: We want them to know that Tahiti is only 7 ½ hours from LA.

The message: Our communication objective, then, is to inform that Tahiti is only 7 ½ hours from Los Angeles.

Once this objective is established, we explore marketing communications *strategies*.

Marketing Communications *Strategies.*

Strategies can be thought of as *ideas.* They can be stale or fresh ideas. Our clients pay us for, and expect, fresh ideas.

Four marketing communications strategies define how we intend to accomplish our objectives:

- Target strategies
- Message strategies
- Mix strategies
- Metrics strategies

Our challenge is to develop and execute ideas about what we will say, to whom, when, where and how we will tell it. This is to achieve an objective of what we want our prospects to do. (Sample the product? Go to a store? Call an 800 number?, etc.)

1. *Target strategy*: Whom are we talking to? If the proper research has been done, we'll know which targets should deliver the best return on our investment. This is called segmenting and prioritizing the targets.
2. *Message strategy:* What are we telling them? What message do we communicate to each target – termed message segmentation. Continuing the example of Tahiti's advertising, we tell the leisure market, "Tahiti is closer than you think."
3. *Mix strategy*: How are we reaching them? The optimum mix between the marketing communications tools of *advertising* (anything that requires paying for the delivery medium), *non-paid*

> (editorial) and *promotions* (offers) needs to be determined.
> 4. *Metrics strategy:* How are we monitoring and measuring the targets' behavior? Are we tracking awareness, preference, behavior and/or sales?

Amplifying further on the three elements of the *Mix Strategy:*

Advertising tools are mediums that are purchased: Media advertising, events, collateral material and interactive devices such as a Web site or a kiosk. The buyer creates the final message and, therefore, maintains control.

Non-paid communications are comprised mostly of media relations and employee relations. The result is editorial content and word of mouth. Therefore, placement and actual content cannot be guaranteed. Non-paid communications most often carry more credibility than paid messages.

Sales promotions are offers to motivate trial or repeat purchases.

The mix of pure brand-building messages, more specific product features/benefits messages and the amount of promotions-based traffic generators will be determined by the objectives.

Pure brand building advertising is often referred to as "image" advertising. However, anything from a big smile from the cashier, to a follow-up "thank you" letter, to a special event can be part of the brand-building campaign.

Here are some general guides for selecting which device to use to achieve the objectives:

(*Note: they are brief and not conclusive, but they add to the logic and completeness of this document.*)

Public Relations: The nomenclature surrounding the various areas of responsibilities for "public relations" can be confusing.

- *Media relations:* Media relations puts editorial messages in the hands of a third party – journalists – whereby placement of the message cannot be controlled or guaranteed. Because positive editorial often indicates the endorsement of an unbiased journalist, it's the great credibility builder. It allows a small company with real news to get attention by spending less than an ad campaign would probably cost. It is a good method for delivering longer messages than could normally be handled in a print ad or 30-second TV commercial. However, if the priority is to create immediate sales, or if you must have tight message and timing control of your message, PR doesn't carry the guarantees that are available from the paid advertising disciplines.

- *Employee relations*: Every employee is a representative of the company – and can be an ambassador. Many have more consumer contact then top management. So, it's important to keep them informed about company vision, policies, communications strategies.
- *Industry relations*: For the same reasons stated for employee relations, it's important to keep suppliers, dealers, retailers – all important links in the trade channels informed.
- *Investor relations:* Informs and educates investors, analysts, brokers and the financial press.
- *Community relations*: Help build images in the company's own neighborhood.

Direct: If the target is identifiable and addressable, if there is an offer that will prompt response, and if the budget allows delivery of a series of packages or commercials, Direct may be appropriate. Direct response media is also excellent for generating a customer relations management (CRM) database.

Because of stockholder demand for ROI, and because technology is making the tracking and reporting of results more feasible, Direct is becoming an increasingly larger part of the marketing mix. The nomenclature can be confusing, so here are the main components of Direct:

- *Direct Marketing:* The marketing and sales functions are one step. The manufacturer sells directly to the ultimate consumers. There are no wholesalers or retailers involved. Examples: Infomercials, catalogs, print ads w/ 800 number and e-commerce.

- *Direct Response:* These messages, whether print or electronic, contain a response mechanism. This response mechanism is usually more than just the mention of a toll-free number. The main purpose and emphasis of the communication is to spur a response action on the part of the audience. While an order is often the preferred response – depending on the distribution channels – other responses are valued for the information that can be used later.

- *Database Marketing:* This is the assembling and use of a list of potential and/or present customers to market products or services. It is not a single action. It's a series of actions, normally with the objective of building a relationship with the customer. It's commonly referred to as "relationship marketing" or as "1-to-1" marketing, and is at the heart of any company's CRM (customer relationship management) program. Demographics, psychographics, and most importantly, purchase behavior statistics, such as recency of last purchase, purchase frequency and average unit of sale, are collected into a database for analysis purposes.

Promotions: Promotions are offers. They're often referred to as sales promotions and are excellent for generating traffic, trial and repeat purchases. Promotions need to be timed and placed correctly. (No one cares about your offer if they don't already desire your product.) With offers, promotions tie in naturally with direct response. A program's ROI is improved by testing the variable of the offer, the target and the message – then by measuring, adjusting and expanding the promotion.

Alliance Marketing: When two or more companies combine funds to deliver messages to the same target, it's called alliance marketing or *partnership marketing.* Alliance marketing works best when companies have similar targets and quality brand images and can result in significantly improved efficiencies. When these partner programs carry an offer, they're referred to as *cross-promotions.*

Advertising: When there is an identifiable target group, when efficient media is available to reach them, when budgets exist to advertise consistently, and when the message can be delivered in small space or in a short amount of air time, advertising will most likely be an important part of the mix. Paid advertising also allows the advertiser to maintain control of content and timing.

Point of Purchase: Referred to as POP or POS for point of sale. Howie Cohen refers to it as "The Closer." It's the last and best chance to close the deal with your target. The other marketing efforts may have brought them to this moment – in the store – in the aisle – approaching your product. You may have excited them with editorial articles, romanced them with tantalizing ads and enticed them with compelling promotions. But if you don't seal the deal with a strong close at the point of purchase, you can lose them. POP is the most effective way to close the deal. When it's possible to get space on the retail sales floor, point of sale is almost always in the mix. It's extremely efficient because the targets are prospects who are in the store and able, at that moment, to purchase the product.

Events: When a group of targeted prospects or customers will be in one place, or when it's economically feasible to bring them together, an event or series of events can be an effective tool. Face-to-face contact can be the most powerful marketing tool. Unsolicited, positive word-of-mouth testimonials from experts may be the most powerful sales tool, and the human contact that takes place at events can approach delivering that level of credibility. Samplings, demonstrations and celebrations are examples of marketing events. Events are also staged to generate publicity.

Product Placement: The use of products by celebrities is a powerful brand-building tool. And as consumers find ways to avoid commercials, as the lines between paid and non-paid marketing communications blur into documercials, infomercials and advertorials, products placed by marketing communications people in editorial and entertainment environments will become more commonplace. (I laugh as I write this because I'm reminded of Mike Meyers, smiling into the camera in _Wayne's World_, holding a bag of chips close to his face, parodying product placement in movies.)

We might wonder if the effort of placing products in an editorial or entertainment environment is to be considered advertising (paid) or public relations (non-paid). Our thinking is that if the producer is paid to include the product in the content – it's advertising. If no fee is paid, it's PR.

A Communications Stream with Three Tributaries.

Here's a template to help with the mental organization of these disciplines or processes: The three basic marcom tools are *advertising*, *public relations* and *promotions*.

1. If space and time are paid for, it's considered *advertising*.
2. If it communicates without paid media, it's *public relations*.
3. If it's an offer, it's a *promotion*.

These messages of the three disciplines, are then delivered by a variety of media vehicles. These delivery vehicles can be organized into three segments: Electronic, print and human contact.

So according to the last chapter, the definition of marketing communications is: *Advertising, public relations and promotions — delivered by electronics, print or human contact.*

That's about as few words as you'll ever see to define marketing communications!

The logic used to determine the efficiencies and effectiveness for using the various delivery vehicles is outlined in the following chapter on media.

Media Strategy.

The overall marcom goal is to reach the right person, at the right time, at the right point of contact, with the right message. So, the essence of a *media strategy* – whether for advertising or for public relations, is to determine:

- Which vehicles to use,
- At what levels of reach and frequency
- In what proportions relative to other mediums
- The best time to use them.

What are points of contact?

People need different information as they move through the various stages of awareness, preference, desire and purchase. A team (especially the media planner, PR person and promotions specialist) will look at these options to get the right message at the right point of customer contact:

- *In home*: print, newspapers, magazines, mail, TV, etc.
- *In transit*: outdoor boards, bus shelters
- *Point of sale:* signage, packaging, demos, kiosks, sampling
- *During use*: inside or on the package, in-flight, on- air promotions, etc.

Another way to look at media options is to divide them into three basic delivery vehicles:

1. *Electronic*: broadcast, satellite, online, kiosks (includes TV, radio, internet)
2. *Print*: newspapers, magazines, outdoor, etc.
3. *Human contact*: sampling, events, telemarketing, trade shows, etc.

How Do We Determine Which Mediums Are Most *Effective*?

Media selection, like message selection, can be as much of an art as it is a science. There are many rules. They're made to be broken if the rationale exists. Exercises to help determine media selection include asking:

- What is our competition using?
- What medium reaches our target that our competition is *not* using?
- How do we get to the target in the right place with the right message at the right time?
- Do we have something newsworthy for the media we want to use?

Here are some factors to consider:

- Will this medium allow delivery of enough information? (Outdoor boards are great, if you can get your message across in seven words or less.)
- Do you need color?
- Do you need room for copy, for features/benefits?
- Do we have dramatic b-roll for news or talk shows?
- Do we have compelling images for editorial that are different than the images used in the ads?
- Where is the individual in the purchase cycle? (Simple iconic branding messages are more meaningful in the early stages of the purchase cycle. Conversely more in-depth copy is often best as interest level heightens – especially on more expensive, considered purchases.

How Do We Determine Which Mediums Are Most *Efficient?*

If we're buying media we ask:
- What percent of the medium's audience is the target?
- What's the cost per thousand, relative to others?
- As we measure behavior, as opposed to awareness and attitude, the cost-per-lead and the cost-per-sale for each medium are important factors.
- What will it take to attain *effective reach* levels? For example, what frequency will it take to change an attitude or create a trial purchase?
- Is the primary objective to create awareness, preference or trigger a response?
- What is the credibility factor for editorial?

For editorial we look at:
- Credibility
- Lead time
- Newsworthiness
- Can we offer what the media needs? (i.e., visuals spokesperson, hot trends, etc.)

In the media neutral environment at The Phelps Group, media relations (PR) and media buying specialists (advertising) share information about which media works best to reach target audiences.

We call this Media^2.

Creative Strategies.

Is it a creative *strategy*? Or is it a strategy for the *creative* message?

The logic we're describing in this chapter is that once we establish who we're talking to and what we want to say, then we develop the strategy for the creative message – which is *how* we're going to say it.

The creative strategy is not the creative concept or execution. It's *how* we are going to say what we want to communicate? For example:

- Will we use endorsements?
- Will we appeal to a sense of fear?
- Appeal to pride?
- Appeal to pity?
- Bandwagon appeal?
- Humor?

There are millions of creative *concepts* that could be used for each of the above strategies.

The targets' characteristics and motivations will guide the best choices.

Remember – it's not often admitted, but quite often the creative *strategy* is written after the creative concept is born. Ideas for creative concepts just seem to pop out at all stages of a campaign's development. If they come in the early stages of plan development – say during research or creation of the general strategies – we always want to capture them, then see how they hold up as we move through the processes. We try not to "fall in love" with our ideas too early in the game.

Once the creative strategies are determined, the concepts can be developed and then, as a safety measure, judged as to whether or not they're on communications strategy.

Interestingly, the creative strategy for media relations is often different because it doesn't target the end consumer. Rather, it is aimed at the editorial gatekeepers – the journalists – who will ultimately talk about the client's product or service. We must be prepared to answer the question, "How will we convince the journalist to cover a story?"

- Is the product truly amazing?
- Does it portend a significant trend?
- Will it educate or inform their readers, listeners and viewers?

- Is it a quirky, fun angle?
- Is there some celebrity or charity connection?
- Does it relate to current events?

Execution: Plans/Tactics.

Strategies lead to tactics, which are described in the plans for each discipline. In order for those plans to be integrated, they must follow the same basic conclusions about the target and the message to be conveyed. Once that's achieved, the following plans can be written:

- Public relations plan.
- Direct response plan.
- Interactive plan.
- Plans for the creative, production and media for traditional advertising.
- Point of purchase plan.
- Packaging.

These plans include deliverables, timeframes and cost.

For example:

- What type of concept is needed for a specific project within the plan: one that promotes an emotional image or one that lists the features/benefits?
- What are the consumer's points of contact for this specific project?
- How do prospecting and acquisition flow to conversion and retention?
- Where is the target (mentally and physically) when they're exposed to the message?
- What's the tone: humorous or serious?
- What's the look: contemporary or classic?
- What determines production values? Time, money and image desired. "Production values" is

Hollywood's term for the quality of the talent, set, film, editing, etc. – and the subject of the next chapter.

Timing is obviously a critical factor in plan development, and is often the downfall of an otherwise good plan. A partial checklist would contain:

- Time for plan development.
- Time for client approvals.
- Time for partner recruitment and their timing needs.
- Time for creative development.
- Time to produce the materials.
- Timing to maximize the buzz.
- Timing for tease campaigns.
- Timing for editorial and ad closes.
- Timing for buy-in by the trade channels.
- Timing for trade shows.
- Timing between paid and non-paid messages.
- Timing for ultimate consumption.

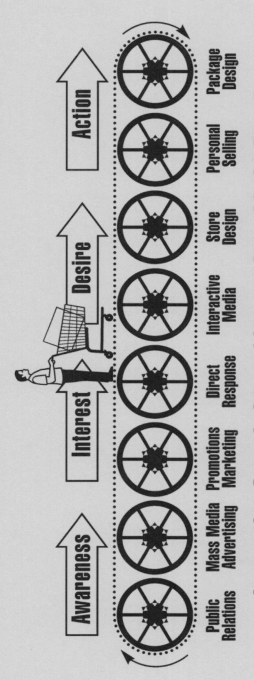

Increasing Association and Interaction with the Brand

Public Relations · Mass Media Advertising · Promotions Marketing · Direct Response · Interactive Media · Store Design · Personal Selling · Package Design

Awareness · Interest · Desire · Action

Concept for this illustration provided by Ed Chambliss, team leader at The Phelps Group.

© The Phelps Group

What Are Appropriate Production Values?

Let's examine "appropriate production values" in more detail, because we're in the midst of much change and debate about this very subject.

Back when Americans had their choice of only three networks, and at the most, six channels in a major market, the audience for each station was huge. Large production budgets for commercials, or elaborate PR stunts for editorial coverage were justifiable because of this.

Fast forward to today, when the average home receives more than 40 channels of TV, and there are thousands of commercial Web sites. Welcome to the age of narrowcasting and "1-to-1 marketing" to different target segments – which calls for many different appeals.

There's a rule of thumb in advertising that no more than 20 percent of the budget should be spent on the creating and producing the message. This leaves 80 percent for the purchase of the media.

And since the cost of creation and production at the highest quality levels is quite expensive, you can see how that 20 percent can get challenged, considering that it now has to cover more projects, or variations on a theme, to appeal to so many markets.

Similarly for editorial, we have to weigh the investment expended to get coverage. It used to be that if you staged an elaborate event and got one or two of the major TV stations to cover it, it was worth it. Today, the viewership of one or two stations may not be worth it. You may be better off creating a video news release (VNR) that is sent via satellite to hundreds of TV stations for the same or less money.

Simultaneously, the sensitivities of the American public to video vs. film are changing. We now have examples of hit movies originating on cheap video that pull in millions of dollars. *The Blair Witch Project* established a new benchmark for films originating on video. "Shaky cam" TV commercials have been around for years. Tons of junky looking stuff on the Internet is considered camp by many. High Definition TV will narrow the gap in resolution between film and video. So, many of the old rules don't apply anymore to production values in advertisements. The same scenario of rapid change applies to print media.

Bet the Farm or Test, Test, Test?

It's always best to start small and roll out. Test in one
market, or one publication, measure response and increase
spending as is practical. However, things are moving so fast
now that there's often no time or money for formal copy
testing research using large sample sizes. The best test of
consumer behavior is response to the actual work. But
often we need some indication of probable success before
we send the message out to hundreds of thousands or
millions of eyeballs.

So, please, those of you at The Phelps Group, listen
carefully to The Wall *, The BrainBangers' Ball , The
Eyeball, your client, your gut, your teammates, your
mother, your kids, your roommate, the cultural
environment of the moment – and, for Pete's sake, the little
voice in the back of your head – because things are moving
so fast, there's most often no time for large-sample-base
research.

*Explained in detail in part two of this book.

Closing the Feedback Loop.

We need to examine the ROI on our programs.

Once the messages are disseminated, we gather input for the next situation analysis, to start the processes outlined in this section from the beginning again.

It's all a learning process. Each loop in the continuous improvement process can be considered a step toward the ultimate product offering and communications program.

Some realities to consider:

- Sometimes the answers come early, which makes the plan easier to write.
- Creative concepts sometime present themselves before creative strategies.
- Sometimes you have a powerful creative concept, but it doesn't follow the most promising strategy. For example, what if it promotes the number two purchase motivator, but it's the most powerful creative concept?
- Do you have the time and money to test it? Do you have the time and funds to measure the ROI, extrapolate the ROI and roll out incrementally?
- How do we measure results of media relations, events and other activities that may not be as easy to track as other activities?

Paid and/or Non-Paid.

True integration means bringing the different marcom disciplines to focus on the same objectives and general strategies. PR, advertising and promotions people are most often trained at companies that specialize in their specific disciplines.

What we know about IMC is that virtually *all the same principles,* and many of the same processes apply, whether we're creating the message ourselves, influencing journalists to publish it or selecting promotional partners or offers.

When communicating to the stakeholders – the investors, employees, journalists, sales force, retailers, influencers and ultimate consumers we must find the answers to:

- Who is the target?
- What do they read, listen to and watch?
- Which of the mediums are the most effective and the most efficient?
- What's the message?
- Is it newsworthy or interesting?
- If not, how do we make it so without compromising the message?

How Do We Determine What the Optimum Marcom Budget Should Be?

One of the most important services we provide our clients is solid advice on how much money is needed to achieve the objectives. Spend too much and there's waste. Spend too little and we may never reach the critical pressure level to achieve results.

Some important questions to answer, and steps to take are:

- What are the supply, demand and awareness levels for the product? And do we have current research in hand to tell us?
- How newsworthy is it?
- How identifiable and addressable are the individuals in our target audience?
- What's the power of the creative? This needs to be tested and measured before we really know.
- What's the cost and power of the offers? This needs to be tested and measured.
- What's the *effective reach* for the message and the medium? We define effective reach as the frequency required to move a consumer to think or do what we've intended. Once this frequency is determined, we determine the reach (size of unduplicated audience) necessary to achieve our volume objectives.

All of the above can best be answered by following these steps:

- Benchmark research.
- Development of alternative campaigns.
- Testing the effectiveness of the media and the message.
- Measuring the results.
- Changing the variables and testing the results.
- Repeating the above steps for continuous improvement.

Searching For the Grail.

Truly integrated programs can deliver *branding* that lives up to its promise by creating a synergy of voices from all marketing communications disciplines – a voice that emanates from one core truth about the product or service. As our agency theme line says: *All communications. One voice.*

We will always be in search of the perfect IMC campaign. Searching for times we have:

- Sent the best message.
- In the right way.
- With the right media.
- To the right people.
- At the right time.
- Enhanced the brand image.
- Increased the sales.
- Increased the profits.
- While we gathered consumer response, and
- Won the big awards contests, and
- Worked as a seamless team with our client, and
- Had fun doing it!

We will always be in search of *talented people:*

- With a strong desire to succeed
- To achieve their client's goals
- And their own potentials
- And cause our agency to be known as:
- "The standard by which all marketing communications agencies are measured."

IMC Feedback Loop

Consumer Information:	Elements of the Marketing Mix		Resources:
	4 P's	4 C's	Client's Funds
Demographics	Product	Consumer Demand	Partner's Funds
Psychographics	Price	Cost	Product Information
Purchase History	Distribution	Convenience	Client / Agency
Motivations	Promotion	Communication	Partner's Personnel

▽

Segmentation Phase 1 ▸ · Competitor's Users · Swing Users · Loyal Customers

▽

Marketing Objective ▸ · Create Trial · Build Loyalty · Build Volume

▽

Communications Objective ▸ Communications Strategy

▽

Marketing Tools ▸ · Advertising · Promotions · Public Relations

▽

Message Delivery Systems ▸ · Electronic · Print · Face-to-Face

▽

Results Short Term ▸ · Awareness · Preference · Sales

▽

Segmentation Phase 2 ▸ Customers

▽

Marketing Objective ▸ Maintain and Build Usage

▽

Marketing Variables ▸ 4 C's and 4 P's

▽

Marketing Tools ▸ · Advertising · Promotions · Public Relations

▽

Delivery Systems ▸ · Electronic · Print · Face-to-Face

▽

Loyal Customers

Feedback

Sales $$$

As Dr. Ed Deming said:

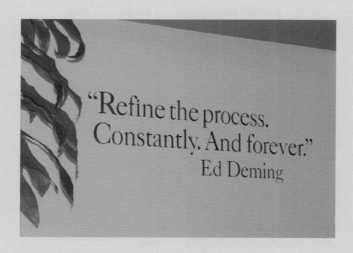

What's the Future For IMC?

The world is *integrating* at the same time it's *segmenting*. It's converging at the same time it's fragmenting. People are becoming more individual in nature as they're becoming more dependent on one another.

Lines are *blurring* (read integrating) between:

- Business and personal life:
  Wireless and free to roam. Work at home. Pets in the office. Company sports teams.
- Between suppliers and customers:
  We sell you products. You sell us information about what you want.
- Between schools and businesses:
  Work study, company-financed education and research programs.
- Between competitors:
  Alliances and co-opetition.
- Between advertising, editorial and education:
  Product placement, advertorials, documercials.

Software is moving toward a common platform and moving closer to the dream of an *enterprise* system that's seamless among all suppliers and our customers.

The Internet is encouraging segmentation that was previously economically unfeasible by aggregating special interests from around the world to become special niche markets with the critical mass to attract companies to supply their demands.

At the same time, the Internet is integrating education, sales, delivery and even maintenance of goods and services worldwide.

Demand is forcing – and technology is allowing – the gradual integration of all elements affecting people's lives.

At some point virtually all of mankind's knowledge and our human desires may be plugged into a worldwide network that reacts dynamically to this knowledge and demand.

"All of us who professionally use the mass media are the shapers of society. We can vulgarize that society. We can brutalize it. Or we can help lift it onto a higher level."

Bill Bernbach

The Proof Is in the Results

The following case histories of IMC campaigns for The Phelps Group's clients illustrate what can happen when marketing communications are integrated to speak with one voice.

Results beyond the ordinary.

☑ Advertising ☑ Public Relations ☑ Promotions ☑ Interactive ☑ Direct Response

+30%
increase in visits

Challenge:
To gain share of visits from bigger vacation destinations such as Hawaii, which outspends Tahiti 30 to 1.

Solution:
Use Public Relations to build image and ads to drive sales. Focus on Tahiti's strength of being the more exotic islands featuring the campaign line, "Tahiti, Islands Beyond the Ordinary." Recruit co-op partners from the hotel, airline, cruise and tour operators to virtually double the media power and reach.

Results:
Visitors to Tahiti from North America have doubled over the past 10 years.

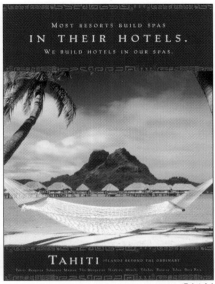

Print Ad

TAHITI
ISLANDS BEYOND
THE ORDINARY

Interactive

Public Relations

Healthy results.

+108%
increase in membership

Challenge:
Create a differentiating brand positioning for Blue Shield 65+.

Solution:
While bigger, more established competitors like Kaiser Permanente and Health Net focused on emotion and made no specific promises, we promoted meaningful "products" for seniors – like smaller deductibles, higher benefits and free rides to the doctor – by featuring them in a fully integrated campaign.

Results:
In just two years, membership grew from 27,500 members to 57,175, a whopping 108% increase. As importantly, the cost per lead from our TV effort was just $80, far below the industry average of $115. Additionally, our direct mail program had an average cost per lead of just $21, which beat the previous control by 15%.

☑ Advertising ☑ Promotions ☑ Direct Response

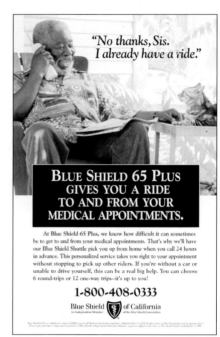

Print Ad

Direct Mail

TV Commercial

282

Results at Web speed.

40% of loan production online

Challenge:
Convince loan brokers using traditional paper transaction processes to try Countrywide's new online processing site, cwbc.com.

Solution:
Focus on brokers' needs for greater flexibility and faster turnaround. Ads featured brokers setting their own working schedules, rather than conforming to a lender's traditional business hours.

Results:
Countrywide achieved a 20% online loan transaction goal just six months after introducing the service – nearly double the annual projected goal. By the end of the first year, online transactions accounted for over 40% of wholesale loan production volume.

Countrywide® CWBC.COM

AMERICA'S WHOLESALE LENDER®

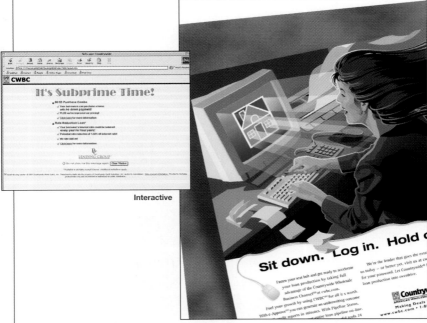

Interactive

Print Ad

Results you can see a mile away.

+20%
increase in market share

Challenge:
To create awareness and sales for the new XTRA-Wide binocular into the college football market during 3rd and 4th Quarter 2000, with a limited budget.

Solution:
A humorous approach that appealed to male sports fans, our primary audience. Additionally, an interactive banner showed the product benefit using limited file space.

Results:
The program helped increase market share from 35% to 42% in a flat market. Sales exceeded projections by 20,000 units for the 5x25 model alone.

Print Ad

Start seeing what you've been missing!

TV Commercial

Animated online advertising

284

Results that will float your boat.

+70%
increase in Web traffic

Challenge:
Already a leader in the luxury cruise market, Crystal Cruises wanted to increase sales to new segments of guests, while lowering costs per guest acquisition.

Solution:
We began with a redesign of Crystal's Web site and online presence. This was supported with acquisition email campaigns, online partnerships and web-based travel agent resources. Existing customer loyalty was addressed with a new online and offline custom publication, *Crystal Cruises' Passport.*

Results:
A significant increase in Web traffic, increased repeat passenger bookings plus significant acquisition of new leads. In addition, the new Web site won a prestigious "Webby" award for excellence two years in a row.

CRYSTAL CRUISES

Luxury on the high seas.

Custom Media

Interactive

285

Results of great interest.

+465%
increase in deposits

Print Ad

Challenge:
To launch a new bank in a cluttered category where there's a major bank on every street corner.

Solution:
Capitalize on IndyMac Bank's technological superiority and cost efficiencies to attract accounts by offering higher CD and Money Market Savings rates. Utilize the theme, "Bureaucracy Beware" to herald a new kind of bank where service still counts.

Results:
The Phelps Group began working with IndyMac Bank in July, 2000. From July, 2000 to July, 2001, the Consumer Bank grew 465%, increasing deposits by over $1.5 billion. By the end of May, 2001, the Consumer Bank had already exceeded their 2001 year-end goals.

We want to be your CD bank.

Bureaucracy BEWARE!™

Make sure you're making the most of your money. One way is to take advantage of stable investments that pay. Like FDIC-insured CDs from IndyMac Bank. We consistently have some of the highest CD rates in the country. And our commitment to service rates just as high. All that plus the safety and security that comes with over $7 billion in assets. Now that's something you can count on.

Covina and West Covina Locations
144 North 2nd Ave. (2nd and College) • 626.331.0651 • Sally Ervolina, Branch Manager
100 North Azusa Ave. (Azusa and Badillo) • 626.967.2829 • Kim Shappell, Branch Manager
255 North Barranca St. (1 block north of 10 Fwy.) • 626.859.4200 • Pam Craig, Branch Manager

IndyMac Bank
www.indymacbank.com

Member FDIC
NYSE:NDE

Yield of Dreams

6% APY www.indymacbank.com
Money Market
$10,000 and up

IndyMac Bank
Bureaucracy BEWARE!

(800) 750-8521

Outdoor

IndyMac Bank®

Enter to Win a Digital Camera From the Bank that Focuses on You.

OLYMPUS

IndyMac Bank

Promotion

LIVE

Michael Perry
IndyMac Bancorp

Public Relations

Results that do the trick.

☑ Advertising ☑ Promotions ☑ Interactive ☑ Direct Response

36 quarters
of consecutive same store sales growth of 5% or more

Challenge:
Establish Petco as the leading authority in the specialty pet category.

Solution:
A strategy of competing directly with supermarkets, which represent a much larger potential for new customers and greater share. TV, direct mail, on-line newsletters and value added affinity programs all targeted "pet pamperers."

Results:
For 36 consecutive quarters, same-store sales for Petco have increased by 5% or more.

Affinity Program

Direct Mail

TV Commercial

PETCO Where the pets go.

Results that improve images.

☑ Advertising	☑ Promotions	☑ Interactive	☑ Direct Response

7.5%	**63%**
response rate	qualified leads

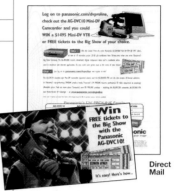

Challenge:
Panasonic needed to give the business customer a compelling reason to choose its Mini-DV camera.

Solution:
Our research revealed that this target audience aspires to greater things. Our communication strategy became "Here's a Mini-DV camcorder that's priced like a consumer model, but shoots like a pro." Three highly targeted mediums were used – print advertising in vertical publications, direct mail with a promotion offer and the Internet.

Results:
Response rate to the direct mail program was 7.5%, from a busy, high-income target. 63% qualified as key-target leads. ROI exceeded projections.

Direct Mail

Web page

Print Ad

Welcome to the big show.

Panasonic® Broadcast & Professional

The Case for IMC

Part Four: A company on a mission

Self-directed teams

operating from a full-feedback environment

delivering IMC

in the spirit of our mission

"Success, like happiness, cannot be pursued; it must ensue ... as the unintended side effect of one's personal dedication to a cause greater than oneself."

Viktor Frankl

The Origin of Our Mission.

Our agency started with the Fender guitar account in 1981.
At that time, I thought our mission might be to sell more
musical instruments than any other agency. But when we
won Baldwin and Gemeinhardt, and were therefore already
serving America's largest guitar and piano and flute
manufacturers, it became apparent that we could go for
loftier goals.

One of our first clients outside the music industry was
Childrens Hospital/Los Angeles. When we acquired CHLA
as a client, we thought, "We only live once. Our work is
only as worthwhile as the clients' products and services we
help sell. So, let's work only for clients whose products
make the world a better place." We called these clients
deserving clients. And the service of these clients is the heart
of our mission.

We are here at The Phelps Group to do great work for deserving clients, in a healthy working environment, to realize our clients' goals and our potentials.

At our 1995 Strategic Advance, we agreed as a group that the definitions of the key components of our mission are as follows:

Great work:

- Builds the brand while generating appropriate sales impact.
- Truthfully communicates the attributes of the product.
- Is delivered on time, on strategy and on budget.
- Uses the mix of disciplines that best suits the clients' needs.
- Generates success that is measurable and for which we can be accountable.

It may also create strategic partnerships for clients at key stages of program development.

In 2002, we agreed to further refine our definition of great work by describing it as work that is a "refreshing jolt to the psyche that gets positive results."

We understand that some great work wins awards. More often, it doesn't. However, the personal satisfaction of doing great work and helping a deserving company succeed is the best reward any career can offer.

If someone asks what we do, a more conversational way to express our purpose might be to say, "We build brands and sales for products that make the world a better place."

For deserving clients:

- Those whose products or services enrich lives and contribute to a better world.
- Those who enjoy mutually rewarding relationships with our associates.
- Those who treat team members and business partners in an ethical manner.
- Those who provide us with honest, timely feedback.
- Those who value our services as an important part of their success.
- Those who strive to allow reasonable time for jobs to be produced in a quality manner.
- Those who allow us to make a reasonable profit on the services we provide.

In a healthy working environment:

- That encourages open, honest and timely communication.
- That requires that we respect each other professionally and personally.
- That allows for balance in our work and personal lives.
- That does not allow for discrimination on the grounds of gender, race, religion, sexual orientation, handicap or age and accords equal treatment to each group member with respect to conditions of selection and opportunities for advancement.

- That provides an aesthetically pleasing, healthful and productive physical workspace that contributes to maximum productivity and bright, positive attitudes.
- That allows the freedom necessary for group members to maximize their personal contributions and, therefore, reap the rewards of personal satisfaction of a job well done.

To realize our clients' goals:

- By enhancing their brand image.
- By building brand awareness.
- By increasing traffic levels, sales and profits.
- By increasing stock value.

And our potentials:

- Requires a commitment by both the agency and the individual toward ongoing personal and professional education and development.
- Requires a constant striving for innovation while providing associates with the best technology available to aid in creating great work.
- Requires challenging ourselves daily by setting, meeting and/or exceeding our goals and expectations.
- Requires utilizing timely and effective feedback at all levels, be it among our associates, with clients or among our peers in the industry.
- Requires fostering of financial success for The Phelps Group and for each associate, as well as an active commitment to company growth, development and perpetuation.

A Thought That's Related to Our Mission.

Some people teach.
Others heal.
Some make roads.
Others make laws.

We are merchants.
That may surprise you.
But that's what we do.
We sell things.

And we can be proud of what we sell.
Because we sell things that
enrich people's lives.

Like education, health care,
musical instruments, sporting gear,
beautiful vacation spots, lovely plants
and other worthwhile products.

So, in effect, through our work
here at The Phelps Group,
we do teach, heal, make music
and help make the world a better place.

Our mission is written on our walls and our business cards.
It adds meaning to our associates' lives and the agency's
existence. We are inspired by it. New associates and clients
come to us because of it.

Part Five: A compelling vision creates alignment and power

Self-directed teams

operating from a full-feedback environment

to deliver IMC

in the spirit of our mission

to achieve our vision.

Aligned for Success.

A company, for ultimate success, can maximize its power by having alignment of strategies in support of its mission, to move it toward its vision to realize its purpose.

Here's our agency's operational philosophy in a nutshell:

Purpose: **To realize our potentials,**

Vision: **We will become the standard for all marketing communication agencies.**

Mission: **We will create great work for deserving clients by:**

Strategy: **finding the right people,**

Strategy: **deploying ourselves in self-directed teams,**

Strategy: **nourishing ourselves with healthy feedback**

Strategy: **and holding ourselves accountable to our own goals.**

Reaching the Potential.

For a company to reach its potential, it must have alignment as to what it's doing, *where it's going* and how it's getting there.

Where a company sees itself going – its Vision – must be clearly understood by each associate. The power resulting from a group of people with a shared vision and values has been shown repeatedly throughout history.

Margaret Mead, anthropologist, said: "Never doubt that a small group of thoughtful, committed citizens can change the world. Indeed it is the only thing that ever has."

Our vision at The Phelps Group is *to be the standard by which marketing communications agencies are measured.* This starts with the individual, flows to the teams, and then to the overall agency. These standards are reinforced with the help of clients, suppliers, friends and family. Here's how we are taking daily steps toward our vision:

Individuals determine where they want to go.

Each associate develops his or her Individual Performance
Objectives (IPO). We suggest taking some quiet time to
think about what's most important to you. Get your nose
off the grindstone. Look longer term at the bigger picture.
Set your goals for the year. State your goals for
contribution to income, contribution to the environment
and for your contribution to the quality of our work.
Clearly outline the intended results, how you expect to do it
and when you'll have it done. Include personal goals, if you
wish. (Often it helps to share these personal goals with
others to create pressure on you to achieve them. For
example, "I'm going to stop smoking.")

Follow up with 1-to-1s.

Progress toward goal achievement is monitored on a
monthly basis in our 1-to-1 meetings. We recommend that
our associates meet monthly with either their discipline
coach or their team leader. For most associates, we
recommend a blend of both throughout the year. It's their
responsibility to schedule these.

The mere reviewing of your goals on a regular basis greatly
increases the likeliness of accomplishment. It's your 1-to-1
partner's job to hold the mirror up so you can see yourself

and your accomplishments clearly. For example, "John I see that you were going to complete a statistics class by next February. How are you doing on that?"

Over the years at The Phelps Group, it's been gratifying to see so many associates setting specific goals. Individually, we're getting more sophisticated in doing this. For some, it's their first time to set individual annual goals in an action plan. Others have been doing it for years, and in some cases, decades.

Associates are encouraged to place their objectives where they can review them daily or, at the very least, weekly. Once individuals have their objectives, the next step toward overall alignment is to ensure that individual goals are aligned with the teams'.

Individual plans flow into team plans.
When the team meets to develop plans for its clients and for the team as a whole, it becomes evident to the individuals if their IPOs are in concert with the team's goals.

We ask teams to agree on what their mission and vision are and specific action steps required to achieve them.

We look to team leaders to make this happen on a client and team basis, answering questions on the team level about how members can best work together on commitments, special procedures and such. And we ask that they develop a plan for each client.

If there's not a written marketing communications plan for each client which contains a situation analysis, conclusions, objectives, strategies and specific executional plans (budget, creative, media, and the involved disciplines) then the team leader is not providing the leadership our clients expect and deserve.

Team plans flow into the agency's plan.

The individual teams' projections, missions and action plans, along with the agency's overall operations plan combine to create the overall plan. When this is shared with the entire group, various individuals volunteer to be team leaders for the agency projects. Then, they present action plans to show when, how and who will make these plans happen.

Alignment with and support of forces outside the team are critical.

Verifying that the individual, team, client and company goals are in alignment is not enough. The company's outside suppliers and the associates' family and close friends are part of the process, too.

We assume that our suppliers have our best interest at heart. In most instances they've proven themselves over time. And we feel that if they have a clear picture as to what our plans are, they're better equipped to help us execute them. They want us and our clients to be successful, so we bring them in for a special evening once a year to have dinner and review our annual plan. Our associates' families and close friends have a strong influence on their attitudes and performance. So, as previously explained, we invite them to a "Mate Night" dinner to review our mission and general plan for the year.

Think of the system as a *rocket*. Each supporting group is like an engine. Get them all lined up in the same direction, reduce drag on the system by eliminating friction caused by lack of information or excess weight, stand back and watch it climb to its full potential.

That's tapping an organization's maximum power.

Spring Advance. Fall Retreat.

Our fiscal year begins October 1. We start the year with a Fall Retreat (and a New Year's party). We retreat to examine our individual needs and aspirations.

The intended result of the Retreat is for all associates to have developed the basis of their IPO for the upcoming year.

We work in small teams and twosomes to help individuals examine the goals the set by asking questions like, "What will you have to give up to make that commitment?"

Annual Advances Are Rocket Fuel For the System.

Prior to our annual Spring advance, we collect the team plans and projections, add them to the agency's new initiatives, and see how it all adds up.

Sometimes it doesn't add up like we want it to. Here's a story to illustrate:

It happened at our agency's 1997 Spring Advance. The expenses for the year were projected. (Salaries, rent and overhead are relatively easy to project. It's the income that's hard to project in our industry.)

As the teams delivered their revenue projections from their team meetings it became increasingly apparent that we were coming up short. We were already in the sixth month of our fiscal year, yet projections were showing us $327,000 short of break-even. For a company of our size at that time, that was a real problem.

As the numbers came in, it was obvious to the associates that I was concerned. (Note: The reason I was so concerned is that I had aggregated every dime of available cash in my estate to make the down-payment on our agency's new building, so there was no cash reserve. Financially, our back was against the wall.)

One person said, "Hey, we can *at least* break even." And the group responded by devising a plan using what we called "stretch goals." There were first level and second level stretch goals.

After the advance, we reported the progress on our stretch goals monthly. And without recommending anything to our clients that we didn't sincerely believe they needed, we ended the year exceeding our basic projections, exceeding our first level stretch goals, and actually making a small profit.

It was confirmation to us as a group, once again, that what we can conceive and believe, we can achieve.

For years now, we've gone away for a Spring Advance. Everyone goes. There's really no way to draw a line and say, "These people stay home; these people go to the Advance." In an organization of self-directed teams, everyone is important. Everyone.

In the beginning, we called them retreats. Once someone said to me, "Joe, a retreat is like a trip to the woods where you have time to reflect. But these aren't retreats, because we work so hard at them." That's true. And some time after that the idea came to call them "Advances." They've been opportunities to get to know each other better. Opportunities to share goals, develop action plans and remind ourselves of what's important to us as colleagues who happen to share a common mission and vision in our professional lives.

Advances are obviously a time to have fun, too. We have some terrific meals together. Many of us – probably at least one-third – are entertainers of some sort – musicians mostly. So there's lots of music, laughter and good cheer. Sometimes we have *too* much fun. We stay up too late, sometimes drink too much, sing too long. And, of course, pay for it the next day.

During the Team Report part of the Advance, we hear what the teams' plans are, where they're going, what their biggest challenges, achievements and failures were in the past year. As the teams report, other teams learn from both the successes and failures of others.

We bring in experts who offer expertise on goal setting, conflict resolution, nutrition, relaxation and stress management techniques such as yoga.

As an agency, our annual Advances have gone a long way toward enhancing the alignment of individuals and teams.

Aligned in Values.

Our work at The Phelps Group influences millions of people daily. Therefore, *truth* is our highest value and our guiding light.

If we're careful to select deserving clients, our task is simply to determine the clearest, most concise way to communicate the truth about their products and services. This is just one more example of how proper alignment of elements adds to the overall power of the organization.

Alignment For the New Economic Order:

To paraphrase Peter Drucker: We're living in an economic order in which knowledge – not labor, raw materials or capital – is the key resource. We're in a social order in which inequality, based on knowledge, is the major challenge.

Some thoughts on this: Our government isn't capable of solving today's social and economic problems. Individuals and companies must contribute significantly to taking care of the less fortunate. Therefore, education, focus and energy are – as usual – the keys to success.

If we align our constant education with working in a learning – and teaching – organization, focused on a worthy mission and operating with high values – we'll be leaders in the new economic order.

Symbolizing Our Alignment.

The five thrusters above our name in our logo represent our five sources of power moving in alignment:

- Organized in self-directed teams.
- In a full-feedback environment.
- To deliver truly integrated programs.
- In the spirit of our mission.
- To achieve our vision.

Measuring Progress Toward Our Vision.

Life is a journey. We will never admit total satisfaction. Therefore, to measure movement toward our goals, we need quantifiable evidence of our successes along the way.

Our feedback devices such as the client, supplier, individual and agency surveys indicate our progress. Our clients' successes and the awards we receive from our industry peers are also indicators of our success.

It's important for people to be able to see their progress – to be able to stop, smell the roses and pop the champagne! Too often, however, company goals are so lofty they're hard to measure. So we've developed strategies and tools for measuring our progress toward becoming *the standard by which marketing communications agencies are measured.*

This chart demonstrates how the individual
processes fit together to create a
results-oriented dynamic marketing
communications environment.

Far better is to dare mighty things, to win glorious triumphs, even though checked by failures...than to rank with those poor spirits who neither enjoy nor suffer much, because they live in a grey twilight that knows not victory nor defeat.

Theodore Roosevelt

Measuring Progress By Our Contributions.

We need *benchmarks* to show progress. These milestones will be expressed as quantifiable *contributions* to our clients, our industry, community, our society and ourselves in general.

Here's the list we've developed of where our contributions will be:

Contributions to *ourselves*:

- Individual and company financial growth.
- Public recognition.
- Editorial coverage.
- Industry rankings.
- Awards.
- Client retention.
- Associate retention.
- Associates' educational levels achieved.
- Our physical well-being.
- Our mental well-being.

Contributions to our *clients*:

- Sales and profits.
- Stock value.
- Brand awareness levels.
- Breadth of IMC services we offer.

Contributions to our *industry*:

- Our innovations in agency organization and processes.
- The publication of this book.
- Volunteers to worthy industry organizations.
- Helping our supplier/partners.

Contributions to our *community* and *society* in general:

- The time we spend lecturing at schools, hosting interns and career day events.
- Our cash, gifts and time donated to charities.
- Our methods of energy conservation and recycling.
- The types of products and services we help sell.
- Our taxes paid.

To help us achieve our goals, we can regularly visualize our contributions to the above contingencies. As a wise person once said, "Those who control the future are those who can best rehearse it."

Anything you can dream,

you can do.

Begin it.

For boldness has power,

magic and genius in it.

Goethe

A Tip on Decision Making.

It's been said, "Life can be best understood looking backwards, but it must be lived forwards."

To illustrate: People probably go to a couple of dozen weddings and funerals in their lifetime. So wouldn't it be smart to learn the proper things to say and do at a wedding and funeral early on in life?

With this thought in mind, here's a tip that may help you make better decisions: If you seem to be having difficulty making a decision, it's probably because you don't have enough information. Once you have enough information, the decision generally becomes easy.

One method I've found for getting a fresh look at a situation is to project yourself into the future a few years, then look back and think about how that decision might have affected your life at that point. Sometimes it sheds new light on the subject. To get even more clarity on this issue, write your own obituary and work back from there.

About the Author – in My Own Words.

My Hermann Brain Dominance test results say that my thought processes are most dominated by the goals and tasks involved in building holistic systems.

This agrees with the drive I have to align the parts of my life into one harmonious organism. As a result, I strive to integrate family, business, religion and leisure time. To me, it all works together for the good. The Japanese term for this is *Zatsing*.

I am a *Pantheist*. I believe that God is not just *in* all things. It *is* all things.

I am a *Meliorist*. I believe that society tends toward improvement, and that human effort can further its improvement.

To me, living "the good life" means living for the ultimate benefit of others while enjoying my stay.

I put that philosophy into my personal purpose and mission, "For my life to have the most meaning, I must

enjoy life as I live it, and help build something that lives beyond me to make the world a better place."

If you've read this book already, you might wonder, "Does this guy live and breath goals, missions, directions, and the integration of strategies and plans?"

Like most people, who I am today, how I think and relate to people, grew out of my early experiences as a child. Here's a little bit about my background that might help explain how my personal philosophy developed.

Much of my early childhood was spent on a farm in Oklahoma in a sort of communal environment. There was my foster father, Daddy Red, his wife, Momma Mae, her brother, Homer, his son, Ronnie, an adopted son, Tuffy, a handy man, Scottie, and me.

Red and Mae also owned a café where farmers met for coffee, and town politics were openly discussed. It was a place where truck drivers and preachers alike dined on chicken-fried steaks and fried okra. This was where I was exposed to a real cross-section of lifestyles.

Everyone on the farm worked in the café with the other employees. I, along with the others, cooked, washed dishes and waited on tables. When it wasn't my turn to work at the café, I was back at the farm fixing fences, hauling hay and doing all the things that were needed to be done on a farm. When the "heat of the day," came, we'd have lunch, nap or play dominoes or cards in the cool shade of the house.

Everyone who ever knew Daddy Red loved him. He created a wonderful atmosphere for the people in the café and on the farm. He enjoyed his work. And despite having only an 8th grade education, he managed to create a wonderful, family-like work environment that mirrors what management experts today might say "empowers" employees to be their best.

The natural system he set up integrated all the essential elements – farm, café, family and community – together. This environment, no doubt, influenced the way I envision the integration of business elements.

Like my Daddy Red, I've always enjoyed my work. Other than a couple of summer jobs working on loading docks in Ft. Worth, Texas, I've never really felt like any job I ever

had was "work." To me, work has always been more like a playground. How can it not be when you follow your heart and do something you're passionate about?

I liked the thrill of making money as a child. So I did what a lot of kids do. I sold things – door to door. Like White Cloverine Salve for fifty cents a tin. "Great for bee stings, sun burns and scrapes." Next, every paperboy's dream job, delivering "The Grit," a weekly newspaper filled with mostly good news and "feel good" stories, like the one about a man who grew a 200-pound watermelon.

In about the 8th grade I started my first band, appropriately named The HairRaisers. I was the drummer. Our second band, Alley Oop, who subsequently became The Cavemen, actually got paid for playing music! Over the years, the bands I played in got better. I started managing my bands, and then other bands, too.

While attending the University of Arkansas in 1971, I had a company called Video-Acts Entertainment. This company was one of the first to use video tape as a sales tool to book bands. By its third year , the company was keeping up to 20 bands a week busy. Networking (another influence from my days on the farm) led to managing a recording studio for a friend, Ben Jack. The integration of the management, booking and recording of the bands just seemed normal to me.

In 1975, while my partner Mike Martin and I were in Los Angeles at *Billboard* Magazine's Talent Forum, we got news that the studio had been struck by lightning and burned to the ground. Fortunately, we were insured, and we converted our part of the settlement to cash, sold the goodwill and moved to California.

Shortly after moving to LA, I became disenchanted with the music business, did some soul searching, and decided to put my marketing degree to good use and experience the corporate world. So I got a job at Grey Advertising, a large corporate advertising company.

My mantra those first few years in advertising was, *"I will learn the science of moving the masses, meet the people I'll work with and find a cause to promote."*

I see now that the "science of moving the masses" in its most sophisticated and powerful state is, in fact, *client-team-based, integrated marketing from a full-feedback environment.* And not only have those of us at The Phelps Group learned it –

we helped *invent* it. I'm still working with people I met those first years, and the "cause" has become promoting our deserving clients whose products make the world a better place.

Regarding goal orientation: In my junior year of high school, I read three books that really lit a fire within me: "Think and Grow Rich" by Napolean Hill and W. Clement Stone; "Psycho Cybernetics" by Maxwell Maltz; and "The Power of Positive Thinking" by Norman Vincent Peale. I definitely bought into Peale's philosophy of "What you can conceive and believe you can achieve!"

Since then, I've had specific goals for the various chapters in my life, and can still recall them word for word. Why not? I repeated them hundreds of times. While in college, my mantra was, *"At the age of 30, I will be the controlling force in a conglomerate corporation, recognized as the leader in entertainment in the Southwest. My income will be $100,000 and I will not slight my family."*

In terms of goal setting, a milestone occurred in my life a few years back, when during our holiday party, the agency presented me with an unexpected gift. The group stood in our living room and recited the agency's mission in unison,

like a classroom would recite the pledge of allegiance –
*"We're here at The Phelps Group to do great work for deserving
clients, in a healthy working environment to realize our clients' goals
and our potentials."*

That was a defining moment for me. For the first time, it
was clear that my goals were the group's goals. The feeling
of camaraderie and alignment for a common cause was
rewarding.

It was a feeling I'd wish for every person – to feel that
you're part of building something worthwhile, and that the
others in your group are with you in your quest to be the
best at what you're doing.

And for just a moment that night, I flashed back to the
days on Daddy Red's farm, and my first memories of
"alignment within an organization." It felt good.

INDEX

Great Society, 13

H

Hartnett, Joe, xii
Humpherys, Bob, xii

I

IBU, 182
Industrial Revolution, 2,
  5, 12, 13, 15
IndyMac Bank
  case history, 285
Information Age, xv
Information Revolution,
  14
Integration, xvii, 139,
  171, 173, 189, 200,
  203, 206, 208, 209,
  210, 213, 222, 229,
  276

J

Jack, Ben, xii

L

Land, Kent, 142
Life training, 147
Lynes, Judy, xii

M

Marx, Karl, 15, 34

Maslow, hierarchy of
  needs, 20
Mead, Margaret, 32, 301
Message segmentation,
  246
Metzger, Jay, xiii
Miyahira, Julie, xiii
MMM. *See* Monday
  Morning Meeting
Monday Morning
  Meeting, 115, 145,
  146, 147

O

Objectives, 43, 80, 188,
  211, 228, 242, 244,
  246, 248, 270, 303,
  304
  (alignment of), 43
  (as part of IPO), 115,
    302
  defined, 235
  marketing, 243, 245

P

Padberg, Nancy, xii
Panasonic
  case history, 287
Peale, Norman Vincent,
  xii
Petco, 192
Petco (cont)
  case history, 286
Peterson, Mike, xiii